WILLIAM INGE

has become world-famous in a few short years.
The insight, compassion and honesty
with which he approaches his stories of small-town
America give them the universality of great art.

Inge cuts directly through the sham and hypocrisy
of middle-class life to lay bare the complex
yearnings, the sufferings and pleasures, the confused
passions and sexual fears which lie
buried in the human heart everywhere.

"A tender and perceptive humanity," says
Tennessee Williams, in his *Introduction*, "shines in
THE DARK AT THE TOP OF THE STAIRS . . .
. . . A world within a world, a true
and wonderful talent."

Plays by William Inge

COME BACK, LITTLE SHEBA

PICNIC

BUS STOP

Published by Bantam Books

the dark at the top of the stairs

A NEW PLAY BY WILLIAM INGE

with an introduction by
TENNESSEE WILLIAMS

Bantam Books New York

THE DARK AT THE TOP OF THE STAIRS

*A Bantam Book / published by arrangement with
Random House, Inc.*

PS
3517
N265
D3
19606

PRINTING HISTORY

RANDOM HOUSE EDITION PUBLISHED APRIL 1958
FIRESIDE THEATRE SELECTION MAY 1958
BANTAM EDITION PUBLISHED SEPTEMBER 1960
SECOND PRINTING
THIRD PRINTING

For

TENNESSEE WILLIAMS

INTRODUCTION

If the writing is honest it cannot be separated from the man who wrote it. It isn't so much his mirror as it is the distillation, the essence, of what is strongest and purest in his nature, whether that be gentleness or anger, serenity or torment, light or dark. This makes it deeper than the surface likeness of a mirror and that much more truthful.

I think the man William Inge is faithfully portrayed in the work of William Inge the dramatist. The perceptive and tender humanity that shines in *The Dark at the Top of the Stairs* is a dominant trait of Bill Inge as I have known him these past fourteen years. Now the American theatre public has begun to know him. When they enter The Music Box Theatre of Forty-fifth Street, west of Broadway, it is like going next door to call on a well-liked neighbor. There is warmth and courtesy in their reception. There is an atmosphere of serenity in his presence, there is understanding in it, and the kindness of wisdom and the wisdom of kindness. They enter and take comfortable seats by the fireside without anxiety, for there is no air of recent or incipient disorder on the premises. No bloodstained ax has been kicked under the sofa. If the lady of the house is absent, she has really gone to baby-sit for her sister, her corpse is not stuffed hastily back of the coalbin. If the TV is turned on it will not break into the panicky report of unidentified aircraft of strange design over the rooftops. In other words, they are given to believe that nothing at all disturbing or indecorous is going to happen to them in the course of their visit. But they are in for a surprise, not a violent one but a considerable one, for William Inge the playwright, like William Inge the gentleman from Kansas via St. Louis, uses his good manners for their proper dramatic purpose, which is to clothe a reality which is far from surface. It is done, as they say, with mirrors, but the mirrors may all of a sudden turn into X-ray photos, and it is done so quietly and deftly that you hardly know the moment when the mirrors stop being mirrors and the more penetrating exposures begin to appear on the stage before you. All of a sudden, but without any startling explosion, it happens, and you're not sure just when and how. This nice, well-bred next-door neighbor, with the accent that belongs to no region except the region of good manners, has begun to uncover a world within a world, and it is not the world that his welcome prepared you to meet, it's a secret world that exists behind the screen of neighborly decorum. And that's when and where you meet the talent of William Inge, the true and wonderful talent which is for offering, first, the genial surface of common American life, and then not ripping but quietly dropping the veil that keeps you from seeing yourself as you are. Somehow he does it in such a way that you are not offended or startled by it. It's just what you are, and why should you be ashamed of it? We are what we are, and why should we be ashamed of it more than enough to want to improve it a little? That's what Bill Inge tells you, in his quiet, gently modulated voice that belongs to no region but the region of sincerity and understanding. No, don't be ashamed of it, but see it and know it and make whatever corrections you feel able to make, and they are bound to be good ones.

X-ray photos, coming out of mirrors, may reveal the ravages of tissues turning malignant or of arteries beginning to be obstructed by deposits of calcium or fat. This is God's or the devil's way of removing us to make room for our descendants. Do they work together, God and the devil? I sometimes suspect that there's a sort of understanding between them, which we won't understand until Doomsday.

But Inge reveals the operations of both these powerful mysteries in our lives if you will meet him halfway, and therein lies his very peculiar talent. You hardly know the revelation has happened until you have parted from him and started home, to your house next door to the Music Box on Forty-fifth Street.

This has a great deal to do with the fact that the very handsome and outwardly serene face of William Inge, the gentleman-playwright, looks a bit older than his forty years.

Take fourteen from forty-four years and you are left with thirty, which was Bill's age when I met him in St. Louis in January, 1945. This was just a few weeks after Laurette Taylor had started breaking the ice of a Chicago winter with her performance, there, of my first success, *The Glass Menagerie*. I had returned to my parents' home in St. Louis as a refugee from the shock of sudden fame, but the flight was not far enough to serve its purpose. I had been home hardly a day when my mother interrupted my work in the basement of our rented suburban home—we had recently ascended from the city-apartment level of economy—to tell me the drama critic of the St. Louis *Star-Times* was on the phone. Bill Inge told me that he also did feature stories on theatrical folk passing through St. Louis and he would like to do a sort of "Home Town Boy Makes Good" article on me. He also wondered, sympathetically, if I would not enjoy a little social diversion other than that provided by family friends in St. Louis, since my own small group of past associates in the city had scattered far and wide, by this time, like fugitives from a sanguinary overthrow of state. He gave me his address and a time to come there. He was living in a housing project, way downtown in a raffish part of the city, but when he opened the door I saw over his shoulder a reproduction of my favorite Picasso and knew that the interview would be as painless as it turned out to be.

After I had gone back to Chicago to finish out the break-in run of *Menagerie,* Bill came up one week end to see the play. I didn't know until then that Bill wanted to be a playwright. After the show, we walked back to my hotel in the Loop of Chicago, and on the way he suddenly confided to me, with characteristic simplicity and directness, that being a successful playwright was what he most wanted in the world for himself. This confession struck me, at the time, as being just a politeness, an effort to dispel the unreasonable gloom that had come over me at a time when I should have been most elated, an ominous letdown of spirit that followed me like my shadow wherever I went. I talked to him a little about this reaction, but I didn't feel that he was listening to me. I think Bill Inge had already made up his mind to invoke this same shadow and to suffuse it with light: and that, of course, is exactly what he has done.

The history of his rise in our theatre is deceptively smooth in its surface appearance, for back of it lies the personal Odyssey of Bill Inge, and in the Odyssey, which I know and which has amazed and inspired me, is a drama as fine and admirable as any of the ones he has given, one after another— an unbroken succession of distinguished and successful plays —to the American Theatre, and someday I hope that he will make a play of it, his personal Iliad and Odyssey, a truly Homeric drama, but one in which the stairs rise from dark to light through something remarkably fine and gallant in his own nature.

TENNESSEE WILLIAMS

Key West
January, 1958

THE DARK AT THE TOP OF THE STAIRS was first presented by Saint Subber and Elia Kazan at The Music Box, New York City, on December 5, 1957, with the following cast:

CAST
(In order of appearance)

CORA FLOOD, *a young housewife*	Teresa Wright
RUBIN FLOOD, *her husband*	Pat Hingle
SONNY FLOOD, *the ten-year-old son*	Charles Saari
BOY OUTSIDE	Jonathan Shawn
REENIE FLOOD, *the sixteen-year-old daughter*	Judith Robinson
FLIRT CONROY, *a flapper friend of Reenie's*	Evans Evans
MORRIS LACEY, *Cora's brother-in-law*	Frank Overton
LOTTIE LACEY, *Cora's older sister*	Eileen Heckart
PUNKY GIVENS, *Flirt's boy friend*	Carl Reindel
SAMMY GOLDENBAUM, *Punky's friend*	Timmy Everett
CHAUFFEUR	Anthony Ray

DIRECTED BY Elia Kazan
SETTING BY Ben Edwards
COSTUMES BY Lucinda Ballard
LIGHTING BY Jean Rosenthal

The home of Rubin Flood, his wife and two children, in a small Oklahoma town close to Oklahoma City. The time is the early 1920's.

ACT ONE

A Monday afternoon in early spring.

ACT TWO

After dinner, the following Friday.

ACT THREE

The next day, late afternoon.

SCENE: *The setting for the entire play is the home of* RUBIN
FLOOD *and his wife and two children, in a small Oklahoma
town close to Oklahoma City. The time is the early 1920's,
during an oil boom in the area. The house is comfortable
and commodious, with probably eight or nine rooms. It is
one of those square, frame houses built earlier in the cen-
tury, that stand secure as blocks, symbols of respectability
and material comfort.*

All we see of the FLOODS' *house is the living room, where
the action of the play takes place. There is a flight of stairs
at the far left. At the top of them is the upstairs hallway,
which is not accessible to windows and sunlight. During the
daytime scenes, this small area is in semidarkness, and at
night it is black. When the hallway is lighted, we can see the
feet of the characters who happen to be there. We are conscious of this area throughout the play, as though it holds
some possible threat to the characters.*

*On the far right, downstairs, is the outside entrance, with
a small hallway one must go through before coming into
the living room.*

*In the middle of the living room is a wicker table and two
comfortable wicker chairs, placed one on each side. Upstage
center are sliding doors leading into the parlor, where we see
a player piano. To the left of these doors and under the
stairway, is a swinging door leading into the dining room.
Extreme downstage left is a fireplace and a large comfortable leather chair. This area is considered* RUBIN'S. *In the
rest of the room are book shelves, a desk, a few small tables
and portraits of* CORA FLOOD'S *mother and father. Through a
large window at the back, we see part of the front porch to
the house, and can see characters coming and going.*

*As for the atmosphere of the room, despite the moodiness
of shadowy corners and Victorian (more or less) furnish-
ings, there is an implied comfort and hospitality.*

*When the curtain goes up, it is a late Monday afternoon
in the early spring, about five o'clock. Outside, the sun is
setting, but the room is still filled with soft, warm light.*

The stage is empty when the curtain rises. CORA *and* RU-
BIN *are both upstairs, he preparing to leave on a business
trip.*

CORA (*Off*) Rubin!

RUBIN (*Off*) Yah!

CORA (*Off*) How many times do I have to tell you to rinse your hands before you dry them on a towel? You leave the bathroom looking like a wild horse had been using it. (RU-BIN *laughs*) I can smell the bay rum clear over here. My! You're certainly getting spruced up!

RUBIN (*Starting downstairs, carrying a suitcase. He is quite a good-looking man of thirty-six, still robust, dressed in West-ern clothes—a big Stetson, boots, narrow trousers, colorful shirt and string tie*) I gotta look good for my customers.

CORA (*Calling down to him*) How long will you be gone this time?

RUBIN I oughta be home end of the week. Saturday.

CORA (*Calling down*) That's better than you usually do. Where will you be?

RUBIN (*Goes to his corner, where he keeps his business para-phernalia*) I've made out my route for ya. I've left it on the mantel.

NEWSBOY (*Calling into house from outside*) Hey, Mr. Flood. Jonsey says your tire's ready at the garage.

RUBIN O.K., Ed, I'll be down to get it.

CORA (*Coming downstairs*) Rubin, you've waited this long to go, why don't you wait now until morning? Here it is al-most suppertime. You won't be able to see any customers tonight, no matter where you go. Wait until morning. I'll get up early and fix you breakfast. I'll fix you biscuits, Rubin.

RUBIN I shoulda been out first thing this mornin'. Monday, and I'm just gettin' away. I can make it to Muskogee to-

night and be there first thing in the mornin'. I can finish
up by noon and then get on to Chicasha.

CORA   I wish you were home more, Rubin.

RUBIN   I gotta make a livin'.

CORA   Other men make a living without traveling all over the
country selling harness.

RUBIN   The way other men make a livin' is *their* business. I
gotta make mine the best way I know how. I can't be no
schoolmaster like your old man was when he brung you
all out here from Pennsylvania. I can't be no dentist like
your brother-in-law Morris. I was raised on a ranch and
thought I'd spend my life on it. Sellin' harness is about
all I'm prepared for . . . as long as there's any harness to
sell.

CORA   (*With a trace of self-pity*)   I envy women who have
their husbands with them all the time. I never have anyone
to take me any place. I live like a widow.

RUBIN   What do you want me to do? Give up my job and
stay home here to pleasure you every day?

CORA   (*She is often disturbed by his language*)   Rubin! Don't
say that.

RUBIN   Jesus Christ, ya talk like a man had nothin' else to do
but stay home and entertain you.

CORA   Rubin! It's not just myself I'm thinking of. It's the
children. We have a daughter sixteen years old now. Do
you realize that? Yes. Reenie's sixteen. And Sonny's ten.
Sometimes they act like they didn't have a father.

RUBIN   (*Sits at table to sharpen his knife*)   You're always
tellin' me how good they do at school. The girl plays the
piano, don't she? And the boy does somethin', too. Gets
up and speaks pieces, or somethin' like that?
(*In* CORA'S *sewing basket he finds a sock on which to wipe
his knife*)

CORA (*Again she is shocked*)   Rubin! Not on a clean sock!

RUBIN   Seems to me you all get along all right without me.

CORA   Rubin, I worry about them. Reenie's so shy of people
her own age, I don't know what to make of her. She's got
no confidence at all. And I don't know how to give her any,
but you could. Her eyes light up like candles every time you
go near her.

RUBIN (*A little embarrassed*)   Come on now, Cora.

CORA   It's true . . . and the boy. Other boys tease him and
call him names, Rubin. He doesn't know how to get along
with them.

RUBIN   He oughta beat the tar outa the other boys.

CORA   He's not like you, Rubin. He's not like anyone I ever
knew. He needs a father, Rubin. So does Reenie. Kids need
a father when they're growing up, same as they need a
mother.

RUBIN   You din allus talk like that. God almighty, when those
kids was born, you hugged 'em so close to ya, ya made me
think they was your own personal property, and I din have
nothin' to do with 'em at all.

CORA   Rubin, that's not so.

RUBIN   The hell it ain't. Ya pampered 'em so much and
coddled 'em, they thought I was just bein' mean if I tried
to drill some sense into their heads.

CORA   Rubin. Don't say that.

RUBIN   You're always kissin' and makin' over the boy until
I sometimes wonder who's top man around here.

CORA   Rubin!

RUBIN   I just said I wonder.

CORA If I kept the kids too close to me, it's only because you weren't there, and I had to have *someone* close to me. I had to have *some*one.

RUBIN You're like an old mare Pa used to have on the ranch. Never wanted to give up her colts. By God, she'd keep 'em locked inside her and make all us men dig inside her with our hands to get 'em out. She never wanted to let 'em go.

CORA (*A little repelled by the comparison*) Rubin, I don't like what you just said.

RUBIN Well, she was a good mare in every other way.

CORA You talk shamefully at times.

RUBIN Well . . . I got my own way of sayin' things and it's pretty hard to change.

CORA (*Watching him primp before the mirror*) You like being out on the road, don't you? You like to pretend you're still a young cowboy.

RUBIN It wasn't a bad life.

CORA Rubin, there are ever so many things you could do in town. Mr. Binny down here on the corner makes a very good living just selling groceries to the neighborhood people. We could find a store like that, Rubin, and the kids and I could help you, too. You'd be happier doing something like that, Rubin. I know you would.

RUBIN Don't tell me how t'be happy. I told you over and over, I ain't gonna spend my life cooped up in no store.

CORA Or a filling station, Rubin. You could run a filling station or a garage . . .

RUBIN God damn it, Cora. I don't mean to have that kinda life. I just wasn't cut out for it. Now, quit pickin' at me. We been married seventeen years now. It seems t'me, you'd be ready t'accept me the way I am, or start lookin' for a new man.

CORA   I don't want a new man. You know that.

RUBIN   Then start tryin' to put up with the one you got.

CORA   I do try.

RUBIN   'Cause he aint gonna change. Kiss me g'bye. (*Playfully rough with her*) You come here and kiss me. (*He grabs her in a fast embrace, and they kiss*)

CORA (*Cautiously*)   Rubin, you've got to leave me some money.

RUBIN   How much you gonna need?

CORA   Uh . . . could you let me have maybe twenty-five dollars?

RUBIN (*Hitting the ceiling*)   Twenty-five dollars? I'm only gonna be gone till Saturday.

CORA   I have a lot of expenses this week, and . . .

RUBIN   *I* pay the bills.

CORA   I take care of the utilities, Rubin. And we have a big gas bill this month, last month was so cold. And Reenie's invited to a big birthday party out at the country club. The Ralston girl, and Reenie has to take her a present.

RUBIN   Me? Buy presents for Harry Ralston's girl when he owns half this town?

CORA   I don't often ask for this much.

RUBIN (*Taking a bill from his wallet*)   Twenty's the best I can do.

CORA   Thank you, Rubin. The Ralstons are giving Mary Jane a big dance. (*Finding a button loose on his coat*) Here, let me fix that.

RUBIN   Cora, that'll be all right.

CORA   It'll only take a minute, sit down. (*They sit, and* CORA *takes needle and thread from her sewing basket*) They're having a dance orchestra from Oklahoma City.

RUBIN   Harry and Peg Ralston puttin' on the dog now, are they?

CORA   Oh, yes. I hardly ever see Peg any more.

RUBIN   I guess they don't have time for any of their old friends, now that they've got so much money.

CORA   Anyway, they've asked Reenie to the party, I'm thankful for that.

RUBIN   The country club, huh? By God, I'd die in the poor-house 'fore I'd ever do what Harry Ralston done.

CORA   Now, Rubin . . .

RUBIN   I mean it. He shot hisself in the foot to collect enough insurance money to make his first investment in oil.

CORA   Do you believe all those stories?

RUBIN   Hell, yes, I believe it. I know it for a fact. He shot hisself in the foot. He oughta be in jail now. Instead, he's a social leader, givin' parties out at the country club. And I'm supposed to feel real proud he invited my daughter. Hurry up.

CORA   I ran into Peg downtown during the winter. My, she was wearing a beautiful fur coat. Gray squirrel. And she was wearing a lot of lovely jewelry, too.

RUBIN   She's spendin' his money as fast as old Harry makes it.

CORA   Why shouldn't she have a few nice things?

RUBIN They tell me they both started drinkin' now. They go out to those country club parties and get drunk as lords.

CORA Peg didn't used to be like that.

RUBIN They're all like that now. The town's gone oil-boom crazy. Chamber of Commerce says we're the wealthiest town per capita in all the Southwest. I guess they're not exaggeratin' much, either, with all this oil money, those damned Indians ridin' around in their limousines, gettin' all that money from the government, millions of dollars. Millions of dollars, and nobody knows what to do with it. Come on, hurry up now . . .

CORA (*Finishing with the button*) Rubin, if you want to make an investment, if you should hear of something absolutely sure, you can take that money Mama left me when she died. Two thousand dollars, Rubin. You can make an investment with that.

RUBIN There ain't no such thing as a *sure thing* in the oil business.

CORA Isn't there?

RUBIN No. Ya can make a million dollars or lose your ass overnight.

CORA Rubin, you don't have to use words like that.

RUBIN I do a good job supportin' ya, don't I?

CORA Of course.

RUBIN Then let's let well enough alone.

CORA I was only thinking, it makes you feel kind of left out to be poor these days.
(*Suddenly, from outside, we hear the sounds of young boys' jeering voices*)

BOYS' VOICES
Sonny Flood! His name is mud!

Sonny runs home to Mama!
Sonny plays with paper dolls!
Sonny Flood, his name is mud!

CORA See there! (*She jumps up nervously and runs outside to face her son's accosters*) You boys run along. My Sonny hasn't done anything to hurt you. You go home now or I'll call your mothers, every last one of you. You should be ashamed of yourselves, picking on a boy who's smaller than you are.
(SONNY *comes running into the house now. It is hard to discern his feelings*)

RUBIN (*Follows* CORA *out to the porch*) Cora, cut it out.

CORA I can't stand quietly by while they're picking on my boy!

RUBIN It's *his* battle. He's gotta fight it out for hisself.

CORA If they touch one hair of that boy's head I'll destroy them.

VOICE (*One last heckler*) Sonny Flood, his name is mud!

CORA I'll destroy them.
(CORA *re-enters the house*)

VOICE Sonny Flood, his name is mud.

RUBIN (*Still on the porch*) Hey, come here, you fat butterball.

BOY Hi, Mr. Flood.

RUBIN How you doin', Jonathan? Let me see how you're growin'. (*He lifts the boy up*) Gettin' fat as a pig. Say hello to your pa for me.
(*The boy runs off and* RUBIN *comes back inside*)

CORA Sonny, did they hurt you?

SONNY No.

CORA   What started it this time?

SONNY   I don't know.

CORA   Did you say anything to make them mad?

SONNY   No.

CORA   They're just jealous because you make better grades than they do. They're just jealous, the little beasts.

RUBIN   Son!

SONNY   Huh?

RUBIN   Want me to teach you how to put up a good fight?

SONNY   (*Turning away from his father*)   I don't think so.

RUBIN   (*To* CORA)   What else can I do? Buy him a shotgun?

CORA   There should be *something* we can do. *Something.*

RUBIN   Everybody's gotta figure out his own way of handlin' things, Cora. Whether he fights or whether he runs.

CORA   I hate for anything to make me feel so helpless.

RUBIN   I gotta be goin'.

CORA   Say good-bye to your father, Sonny.

RUBIN   (*Making a point of being friendly*)   Good-bye, son.

SONNY   (*Diffidently*)   G'bye.

RUBIN   (*Giving up*)   Oh, hell.

CORA   Isn't there anything you can say to him?

RUBIN   Cora, if that boy wants me to help him, he's gotta come to me and tell me how. I never know what's on his mind.

CORA   You're just not interested.

RUBIN   Oh, hell, I give up. I plain give up.
(*Exasperated,* RUBIN *bolts outside,* CORA *anxiously following him to the door*)

CORA   Rubin . . . Rubin . . . (*We hear* RUBIN'S *car drive off.* CORA *comes back inside*) Why don't you listen to your father, Sonny? Why don't you let him help you?

SONNY   Where's Reenie?

CORA   She's downtown. Your father isn't here very often. Why don't you try and get along with him when he is?

SONNY   (*Wanting to evade the issue*)   I don't know.

CORA   Most boys your age *worship* their fathers.

SONNY   I like him, all right. Where are my movie stars?

CORA   Forget your movie stars for a minute. You have a father to be proud of, Sonny. He and his family were pioneers. They fought Indians and buffalo, and they settled this country when it was just a wilderness. Why, if there was a movie about them, you couldn't wait to see it.

SONNY   Mom, it just makes it worse when you come out and tell those boys you're going to call their mothers.

CORA   You just won't listen to me, will you? You just won't listen to anyone. You're so set in your ways.

SONNY   I want my movie stars.

CORA   I put them in the book shelves when I was straightening up this morning. The only pastime you have is coming home here and playing with those pictures of movie stars. (SONNY *gets out his scrapbook and spreads it on the floor*)

SONNY   I like them.

CORA   That's all the friends you have. Not real friends at all. Just *pictures* of all the lovely friends you'd *like* to have.

There's a mighty big difference between pictures of people and the way people really are.

SONNY   I like pictures.

CORA   Maybe you should get out and play with the other boys more often, Sonny.

SONNY   They play stupid games.

CORA   People distrust you if you don't play the same games they do, Sonny. It's the same after you grow up.

SONNY   I'm not going to play games just to make them like me.

CORA   (*Suddenly warm and affectionate*)   Come to me, Sonny. I wish I understood you better, boy.

SONNY   I don't see why.

CORA   (*Caressing him*)   No, I don't suppose you do. You're a speckled egg, and the old hen that laid you can't help wondering how you got in the nest. But I love you, Sonny. More than anything else in the world.

SONNY   Mom, can I go to a movie tonight?

CORA   You know the rules. One movie a week, on Friday night.

SONNY   Please, Mom. It's a real special movie tonight. Honest, I just *got* to see it.

CORA   Oh, I bet. It's always something special and you've just got to see it like your very life depended on it. No. You're supposed to study on week nights. Now, stay home and study.

SONNY   I've already got all my lessons.

CORA   You have to speak at Mrs. Stanford's tea party next Saturday. Why don't you memorize a new recitation?

SONNY   I can't find anything I like.

CORA   Oh! I found a cute little poem in the Oklahoma City
paper this morning. It's about a little boy who hates to
take castor oil. It starts off:
"Of all the nasty things, gee whiz!
I think the very worst there is . . ."

SONNY   (*Obviously bored*)   I want to do something serious.

CORA   Serious! Like what?

SONNY   I dunno.

CORA   Goodness, it seems to me we've got enough serious
things in the world without you getting up to recite sad
pieces.
(*Outside the window, we see* FLIRT *and* REENIE *come onto
the porch, giggling*)

SONNY   I'm tired of all those stupid pieces you cut out of
the papers.

CORA   My goodness! Aren't we getting superior! Oh, here's
your sister, Sonny. Be a little gentleman and open the
door for her.

REENIE   (*Sticking her head in through the door, asking cautiously*)   Is Daddy gone, Mom?

CORA   Yes, he's gone. The coast is clear.

REENIE   (*Runs to* CORA *excitedly. She is a plain girl with no
conscious desire to be anything else*)   Oh, Mom, it's the
prettiest dress I ever had.

CORA   Bring it in.

REENIE   Come on in, Flirt.

FLIRT   (*Enters carrying a large dress box. She is a vivacious
young flapper of the era*)   Hello, Mrs. Flood.

CORA   Hello, Flirt.
  (FLIRT *opens the box*)

REENIE   And they took up the hem and took in the waist so that it fits me just perfectly now.

FLIRT   I think it's simply scrumptious, Mrs. Flood.

CORA   Thank you, Flirt. Hold it up, Reenie.

FLIRT   Yes, hold it up.

REENIE   (*Holding the dress before her*)   Is Dad going to be awfully mad, Mom?

CORA   I told you, he's not going to know anything about it for a while, Reenie. He gave me some money before he left, enough for me to make a small down payment. My, I bet Flirt thinks we're terrible, plotting this way.

FLIRT   Shucks, no. Mama and I do the same thing.

REENIE   Oh, Mom. You should see the dress Flirt got.

FLIRT   It's all red, with spangles on it, and a real short skirt. It's just darling. Daddy says he feels like disowning me in it.

CORA   Did you buy your dress at Delman's, too, Flirt?

FLIRT   (*She can't help boasting an advantage*)   No. Mama takes me into Oklahoma City to buy all my clothes.

CORA   Oh!

SONNY   (*Feeling the dress*)   Look, it's got stars.

REENIE   (*Snapping angrily*)   Sonny, take your dirty hands off my new dress.

SONNY   (*Ready to start a fight any time* REENIE *is*)   My hands are *not* dirty! So there.

REENIE   You make me mad. Why don't you go outdoors and play ball instead of staying in the house all the time, spying on everything I do. Mother, why don't you make him go out and play?

SONNY   It's my house as much as it's yours, and I've got as much right to be here as you do. So there!

CORA   (*Always distressed by their fighting*)   Reenie. He only wanted to touch the dress. He likes pretty things, too.

FLIRT   Gee whiz, he hasn't done anything, Reenie.

CORA   Of course he hasn't. You kids are just antagonistic to each other. You scrap all the time.

SONNY   I hate you.

REENIE   I hate you, too.

CORA   Now stop that. Is that any way for a brother and sister to talk? I'm not going to have any more of it. Flirt, are you taking the Ralston girl a birthday present?

FLIRT   Mama got me a compact to give her. It's the only thing we could think of. She already has everything under the sun.

CORA   Yes, I suppose so. Her parents are so wealthy now. Well, I'll have to shop for something for Reenie to take her.

FLIRT   You know, my folks knew the Ralstons before he made all his money. Mama says Mrs. Ralston used to clerk in a millinery store downtown.

CORA   Yes, I knew her then.

FLIRT   And my daddy says that Mr. Ralston was so crazy to make money in oil that he shot himself in the foot. Isn't that awful?

SONNY   Why did he do that?

(REENIE *goes into the parlor to try on her dress.* SONNY *sits at the table.* FLIRT *fascinates him*)

FLIRT   So he could collect enough insurance money to make his first investment in oil. Did you hear that story, too, Mrs. Flood?

CORA   Oh, yes . . . you hear all kinds of stories about the Ralstons now.

FLIRT   And you know, some of the women out at the country club didn't want to give Mr. Ralston a membership because they disapproved of *her*.

CORA   Is that so?

FLIRT   But when you've got as much money as the Ralstons do, I guess you can be a member of *any*thing. I just hate Mary Jane Ralston. Some of the boys at school think she's pretty but I think she's a *cow*. I'm not being jealous, either. I guess if I had as much money to spend on clothes as she does, I'd have been voted the prettiest girl in school, too. Anyway, I'm absolutely positive she peroxides her hair.

CORA   Really?

REENIE (*Poking her head out between the sliding doors*) Are you sure?

FLIRT   Yes. Because she and I play on the same volley ball team in gym class, and her locker is right next to mine, and . . .

CORA (*Reminding her of* SONNY'S *presence*) Flirt!

FLIRT   Isn't it terrible for me to say all these things, when I'm going to her birthday party? But I don't care. She just invited me because she had to. Because my daddy's her daddy's lawyer.

SONNY (*As* REENIE *comes out of parlor wearing her new dress, he makes a grotesque face and props his feet on the table*) Ugh . . .

CORA   Oh, Reenie! it's lovely. Sonny, take your feet down. Let me see! Oh, Reenie. He did a fine job. Flirt! tell me more about the young man who's taking Reenie to the party.

FLIRT   He's a Jew, Mrs. Flood.

CORA   Oh, he is?

REENIE   Do you think it's all right for me to go out with a Jew, Mom?

CORA   Why, of course, dear, if he's a nice boy.

FLIRT   His name is Sammy Goldenbaum, and he comes from Hollywood, California, and his mother's a moving-picture actress.

CORA   Really?

REENIE   Flirt just found that out, Mom. I didn't know it before.

SONNY (*All ears*)   A moving-picture actress!

FLIRT   Yes, but she just plays itsy-bitsy parts in pictures. I saw her once. She played a real stuck-up society woman, and she was Gloria Swanson's rival. You see, they were in love with the same man, Thomas Meighan, and she told all these lies about Gloria Swanson to make people think Gloria Swanson wasn't nice, so she could marry Thomas Meighan herself. But Thomas Meighan found out all about it, finally, and . . .

REENIE   Mom, what's a Jewish person like?

CORA   Well, I never knew many Jewish people, Reenie, but . . .

FLIRT   I've heard that some of them can be awful fast with girls.

CORA   I'm sure they're just like any other people.

FLIRT   (*Dancing coquettishly about room*) They don't believe in Christianity.

CORA   Most of them don't.

REENIE   But do they act different?

CORA   (*Not really knowing*) Well . . .

FLIRT   My daddy says they always try to get the best of you in business.

CORA   There are lots of very nice Jewish people, Reenie.

FLIRT   Oh, sure! Gee whiz, of course.

REENIE   I don't know what to expect.

FLIRT   Kid, he's a *boy*. That's all you have to know.

CORA   There are Jewish families over in Oklahoma City, but I guess there aren't any here in town.

FLIRT   Oh, yes there are, Mrs. Flood. The Lewises are Jewish, only they changed their name from Levin so no one would know.

CORA   I guess I did hear that some place.

REENIE   Mom, I feel sort of scared to go out with someone so different.

FLIRT   (*She never seems aware of her casual offensiveness*) Oh, you're crazy, Reenie. Gee whiz, I'd never go steady with a Jewish boy, but I'd sure take a date with one—if I didn't have any other way of going.

CORA   Now, Reenie, I'm sure that any friend of the Givens boy is nice, whether he's Jewish or not. And besides, his mother's a movie actress. Think of that.

FLIRT Yes, but not a famous one.

CORA (*To* REENIE) Now, you have a nice date to the party, and a lovely new dress to wear. You can be sure you'll have a good time.

FLIRT Gosh, yes! After all, a party's a party. And it's out at the country club, and they're having a swell dance orchestra from Oklahoma City, and they're giving favors. I can't wait. Fix your hair real cute and you'll look all right. (*Looks at her wrist watch*) Oh, heck! I've got to go home.

CORA Do you want to stay here for supper, Flirt?

FLIRT No. It's my night to fix supper for the folks. My mother makes me fix supper once a week, cook's night out. She says it's good for me to learn something about home-making. Isn't that crazy? The only thing I know how to cook is salmon loaf. I learned how to make it in domestic science class. I've made salmon loaf every Monday night now for the whole year. Kid, can you help me study for that stupid old civics test we're having next week?

REENIE I guess so.

FLIRT Civics! Why can't they teach us something in that old school that'd do us some good?

CORA Good-bye, Flirt.

FLIRT Good-bye, Mrs. Flood, good-bye, Reenie. Oh, Sonny, you come over to *my* house and play sometime. I know how to be nice to little boys.

CORA Good-bye! (FLIRT *exits*) Sonny, you've got to go to the store now if we're going to have anything for supper tonight.

SONNY Mom! Can I get a candy bar?

CORA Wouldn't you rather have the nickel to put in your piggy bank?

SONNY   No—I want a candy bar.

CORA   All right. If you promise not to eat it before supper.

REENIE   I want one, too. I want a nut Hershey.

CORA   Bring one for Reenie, too.

SONNY   She can get her own candy bar.

REENIE   He's mean, Mom.

SONNY   I don't care. She makes me mad, and I don't like her.

CORA   Sonny, she's your sister.

SONNY   I don't care. I don't like her.
    (*He exits*)

CORA   Oh, God, some day you kids are going to be sorry.
When you can't even get along with people in your own
family, how can you expect to get along with people out
in the world? (*Goes to the window and looks out, protectively*) Poor Sonny, every time he leaves the house, those
neighborhood bullies pick on him. I guess they've all gone
home now.
    (REENIE *takes off her new dress and throws it on a chair*)

REENIE   I don't know if I like Flirt or not.

CORA (*Comes away from the window*) Why, what's the
matter?

REENIE   The only reason she likes me is because I help her
with her studies.
    (REENIE *goes into the parlor, gets her daytime clothes,
and comes back into the living room to put them on*)

CORA   Why do you say that?

REENIE   I just do.

CORA   You don't think *anyone* like you, do you?

REENIE   Mom, maybe we shouldn't have bought the dress.

CORA   What?

REENIE   I mean it, Mom. Dad'd be awful mad if he knew.

CORA   I told you, he's not going to know.

REENIE   Won't he be here the night of the party?

CORA   No. And even if he were, he wouldn't notice the dress was new unless you told him about it.

REENIE   Just the same, Mom, I don't feel right about it.

CORA   Why don't you feel right?

REENIE   Because . . . the dress cost so much, and what good is it going to do me? I never have a good time at those dances, anyway. No one ever dances with me.

CORA   This time it's going to be different. You've got a new dress, and you've got a nice young man coming here all the way from California to be your escort. Think of it. Why, most young girls would be too excited to breathe.

REENIE   It's just a *blind* date.

CORA   What are you talking about?

REENIE   They give blind dates to all the girls in town that nobody else wants to take.

CORA   Daughter, I'm sure that's not so.

REENIE   Oh, Mom, you just don't know.

CORA   I do too.

REENIE   Besides, he's Jewish. I never knew a Jewish boy before. I'm scared.

CORA   Daughter, you're just looking for excuses. You just

don't want to go, do you? Reenie, don't you want to have friends?

REENIE   Yes, but . . .

CORA   You're not going to make friends just staying home playing the piano, or going to the library studying your lessons. I'm glad you're studious and talented, but those things aren't enough just in themselves.

REENIE   I don't want to talk about it any more.

CORA   You're going to have to talk about these things some-day. Where are you going?

REENIE   To practice the piano.
(*She goes into the parlor and starts playing scales*)

CORA   (*Angrily impatient*)   That's where you spend half your life, *practicing* at the piano. (REENIE *bangs on piano exasperatedly and exits to dining room*) But will you get up and play for people so they'll know how talented you are? No. You hide your light under a bushel. You stay home and play behind closed doors, where no one can hear you except your own family. All you do is *pity* yourself at the piano. That's all. You go in there and pity yourself, play-ing all those sad pieces.
(REENIE *comes out of dining room, and calms herself by watering her plants*)

REENIE   Mom, I just couldn't get up before an audience and play. I just couldn't.

CORA   Why couldn't you? What good is it for your father to have bought the piano? What use is it? (REENIE *begins to sob*) Now, don't cry, Reenie. I'm sorry. (REENIE *goes into parlor and resumes her monotonous scales*. CORA *goes to telephone*) Long distance? Give me three-six-oh-seven-J in Oklahoma City, please. (*There is a wait of several mo-ments*) Hello, Lottie. . . . Lottie, can you and Morris come over to dinner Friday night? I haven't seen you for so long, I want to talk with you, Lottie. I've just got to see some of my own flesh and blood. (*We hear* RUBIN'S *car*

*slam to a stop outside; the car door slams and then he
comes stomping up to the front porch)* Reenie's going to a
big party out at the country club, and I thought I'd have a
nice dinner first. . . . Rubin won't be here and I'll want
company. Please come. Oh, I'm so glad. I'll be looking
forward to seeing you.

RUBIN *(Bursting into the house)* What the hell's been goin'
on behind my back? *(Sees the innocent dress lying on
a chair)* There it is!

CORA *(Her phone call over)* Rubin!

RUBIN *(Displaying the dress as evidence)* So this is what ya
wanted the extra money for. Fine feathers! Fine feathers!
And ya buy 'em when my back is turned.

CORA Rubin, we were going to tell you. . . .

RUBIN A man has t'go downtown and talk with some of his
pals before he knows what's goin' on in his own family.

CORA Who told you?

RUBIN That's all right who told me. I got my own ways a
findin' out what goes on when my back is turned.

CORA You didn't leave town at all. You've been down to that
dirty old pool hall.

RUBIN I got a right to go to the pool hall whenever I damn
please.

CORA I thought you were in such a hurry to get out of town.
Oh, yes, you had to get to Muskogee tonight.

RUBIN I can still make it to Muskogee. *(Finds the price tag
on the dress)* Nineteen seventy-five! Lord have mercy!
Nineteen seventy-five.

CORA Did Loren Delman come into the pool hall while you
were there? Did he? Did he tell you? If he did I'll never
buy anything in that store again.

RUBIN   That'd suit me just fine.

CORA   Oh, why couldn't he have kept his mouth shut? I was going to pay for the dress a little at a time, and . . .

RUBIN   "The finest dress I had in the store," he says, walkin' into the Arcade with a big cigar stuck in his mouth, wearin' a suit of fine tailored clothes. "I just sold your wife the finest dress I had in the store."

CORA   Oh, that makes me furious.

RUBIN   Jesus Christ, woman, whatta you take me for, one a those millionaire oil men? Is that what you think you're married to?

REENIE   (*Pokes her head in through parlor door, speaking with tears and anxiety*)   I told you he'd be mad, Mom. Let's take the dress back, Mom. I don't want to go to the party anyhow.

CORA   (*Angrily impatient*)   Get back in that parlor, Reenie, and don't come in here until I tell you to.
    (CORA *slams the parlor doors shut*)

RUBIN   See there! That girl don't even want the dress. It's *you*, puttin' all these high-fallutin' ideas in her head about parties, and dresses and nonsense.

CORA   Rubin, of course Reenie doesn't want to go to the party. She never wants to go any place. All she wants to do is lock herself in the parlor and practice at the piano, or go to the library and hide her nose in a book. After all, she's going to want to get married one of these days, isn't she? And where's she going to look for a husband? In the public library?
    (RUBIN *goes to his corner, sits in his big leather chair, and draws a pint of whiskey out of his desk drawer*)

RUBIN   I bought her a fine dress . . . just a little while back.

CORA   Oh, you did?

RUBIN Yes, I did.

CORA That's news to me. When?

RUBIN Just a few months ago. Sure I did.

CORA I certainly never saw it. What'd it look like?

RUBIN It was white.

CORA Rubin Flood, that was the dress you bought her three
years ago when she graduated from the eighth grade. And
she hasn't had a new dress since then, except for a few
school clothes.

RUBIN Why couldn't she wear the white dress to the party?

CORA Because she's grown three inches since you got her
that dress, and besides I cut it up two years ago and dyed
it black and made her a skirt out of it to wear with a
middy.

RUBIN Just the same, I ain't got money to throw away on
no party togs. I just ain't got it.

CORA Oh, no. You don't have money when we need something here at home, do you?

RUBIN I'm tellin' ya, right now I don't.

CORA But you always have money for a bottle of bootleg
whiskey when you want it, don't you? And I daresay
you've got money for a few other things, too, that I
needn't mention just at present.

RUBIN What're ya talkin' about?

CORA *You* know what I'm talking about.

RUBIN The hell I do.

CORA I know what goes on when you go out on the road.
You may tell me you spruce up for your customers, but I
happen to know better. Do you think I'm a fool?

RUBIN   I don't know what you're talkin' about.

CORA   I happen to have friends, decent, self-respecting people, who tell me a few things that happen when you visit Ponca City.

RUBIN   You mean the Werpel sisters!

CORA   It's all right, who I mean. I have friends over there. That's all I need to say.

RUBIN   Those nosy old maids, the Werpel sisters! God damn! Have they been runnin' to you with stories?

CORA   Maybe you don't have money to buy your daughter a new dress, but it seems you have money to take Mavis Pruitt to dinner whenever you're over there, and to a movie afterwards, and give her presents.

RUBIN   I've known Mavis . . . Pruitt ever since I was a boy! What harm is there if I take her to a movie?

CORA   You're always too tired to take *me* to a movie when you come home.

RUBIN   Life's different out on the road.

CORA   I bet it is.

RUBIN   Besides, I din ask her. She come into the Gibson House one night when I was havin' my dinner. What could I do but let her join me?

CORA   She went to the Gibson House because she knew *you* were there. I know what kind of woman she is.

RUBIN   She's not as bad as she's painted. That poor woman's had a hard time of it, too.

CORA   Oh, she has!

RUBIN   Yes, she has. I feel sorry for her.

CORA   Oh, you do!

RUBIN   Yes, I do. Is there any law that says I can't feel sorry for Mavis Pruitt?

CORA   She's had her eye on you ever since I can remember.

RUBIN   Oh, shoot!

CORA   What happened to the man she left town with after we were married?

RUBIN   He run off and left her.

CORA   For good reason, too, I bet. I also heard that she was seen sporting a pair of black-bottom hose shortly after you left town, and that you were seen buying such a pair of hose at the Globe Dry Goods Store.

RUBIN   By God, you got yourself a real detective service goin', haven't you?

CORA   I don't ask people to tell me these things. I wish to God they didn't.

RUBIN   All right. I bought her a pair of hose. I admit it. It was her birthday. The hose cost me sixty-eight cents. They made that poor woman happy. After all, I've known her ever since I was a boy. Besides, I was a li'l more flush then.

CORA   How do you think it makes me feel when people tell me things like that?

RUBIN   Ya oughtn'ta listen.

CORA   How can I help it?

RUBIN   (*He has to stop to remember to call Mavis Pruitt by her full name, to keep* CORA *from suspecting too much familiarity between them*)   There's nothin' 'tween me and Mavis . . . Pruitt . . . Mavis Pruitt, nothin' for you to worry about.

CORA   There's probably a woman like her in every town you visit. That's why you want to get out of town, to go frisking over the country like a young stallion.

RUBIN   You just hush your mouth. The daughter'll hear you.

CORA   (*Indulging in a little self-pity*)   A lot you care about your daughter. A lot you care about any of us.

RUBIN   You don't think I care for ya unless I set ya on my knee and nuzzle ya.

CORA   What you need for a wife is a squaw. Why didn't you marry one of those Indian women out on the reservation? Yes. She'd make you rich now, too, wouldn't she? And you wouldn't have to pay any attention to her at all.
(SONNY *is seen coming onto porch*)

RUBIN   All right. Maybe that's what I *shoulda* done.

CORA   Oh. So you want to throw it up to me!

RUBIN   Throw what?
(SONNY *quietly enters the room, carrying a sack of groceries.* CORA *and* RUBIN *are too far into battle to notice him*)

CORA   You know what, Rubin Flood.

RUBIN   I don't know nothin'.

CORA   You never *wanted* to marry me.

RUBIN   I never said that.

CORA   It's true, isn't it?

RUBIN   I'm tellin' ya, it ain't.

CORA   It is. I've felt it all these years.
(SONNY *crosses and goes through the parlor into the dining room, still unobserved by* RUBIN *and* CORA)

RUBIN   All right. If you're so determined to think it, then go ahead. I admit, in some ways I din wanna marry nobody. Can't ya understand how a man feels, givin' up his freedom?

CORA   And how does a woman feel, knowing her husband married her only because . . . because he . . . (CORA *now spots* REENIE *spying between the parlor doors. She screams at her*) Reenie, get away from there!

RUBIN   None of this is what we was arguin' about in the first place. We was arguin' about the dress. Ya gotta take it back.

CORA   *I won't.*

RUBIN   *Ya will.*

CORA   Reenie's going to wear her new dress to the party, or you'll have to bury me.

RUBIN   You'll take that dress back to Loren Delman, or I'm leavin' this house for good and never comin' back.

CORA   Go on. You're only home half the time as it is. We can get along without you the rest of the time.

RUBIN   Then that's what you're gonna do. There'll be ice-cream parlors in hell before I come back to this place and listen to your jaw.
(*He bolts into the hallway*)

CORA   Get out! Get out and go to Ponca City. Mavis Pruitt is waiting. She's probably getting lonesome without you.
(SONNY *quietly enters from the dining room, and watches*)

RUBIN   By God, Cora, it's all I can do to keep from hittin' you when you talk like that.

CORA   (*Following him into hallway, taunting him. Here they are both unseen by audience*)   Go on and hit me! You wouldn't dare! (*But he does dare. We hear the sound of his blow, which sends* CORA *reeling back into parlor*) Rubin! (*Reenie watches from the parlor.* SONNY *is still in the living room*)

RUBIN   I'll go to Ponca City, and drink booze and take Mavis to the movies, and raise every kind of hell I can think of. T'hell with you!
(*He bolts outside*)

CORA   (*Running to the door*)   Don't you ever set foot in this house again, Rubin Flood. I'll never forget what you've said. Never! Don't you ever come back inside this house again!
(*We hear* RUBIN'S *car drive off now.* CORA *returns to the living room, still too dazed to be sure what has happened*)

SONNY   Gee, Mom. That was the worst fight you ever had, wasn't it?

CORA   How long have you been standing there, Sonny?

SONNY   Since he hit you.

REENIE   (*Coming forth*)   Did he mean it about not coming back? Oh, Mom, why did you have to say all those things? I love Daddy. Why do you say those things to him?

CORA   Oh, God, I hate for you kids to see us fight this way.

SONNY   What did he mean, he didn't want to marry you?

CORA   You're not old enough to understand these things, Sonny.

SONNY   Did he hurt you, Mom. Did he?

CORA   I'm still too mad to know whether he did or not.

REENIE   I don't think he'll ever come back. What'll we do, Mom?

CORA Now, don't worry, Reenie.

REENIE Will we have to go to the poorhouse?

CORA No, of course not. Now, quit worrying.

REENIE But if Daddy doesn't come back?

CORA I still have the money my mother left me, haven't I?
And if worst comes to worst we can always go to Oklahoma
City and move in with your Aunt Lottie and Uncle
Morris.

SONNY (*Jumping up and down in glee*) Goody, goody,
goody. I wanta move to Oklahoma City.

REENIE Listen to him, Mom. He's *glad* Daddy's gone. He's
glad.

SONNY I don't care. I wanta move to Oklahoma City.

REENIE I don't. *This* is home. *This* is. And I don't want to
move.

CORA Now, children!

REENIE I hate you.

SONNY I hate you, too. So there! Oklahoma City! Oklahoma City! I wanta move to Oklahoma City!

CORA Stop it! There's been enough fighting in this house for
one night. Reenie, take your dress upstairs and hang it in
the closet.

REENIE I hate the old dress now. It's the cause of all the
trouble. I hate it.

CORA You do what I tell you. You take that dress upstairs
and hang it in the closet. You're going to go to that party if
I have to take you there myself. (REENIE *starts upstairs*)

The next time you're invited to a party, I'll let you go in a hand-me-down.

SONNY (*With the joy of discovering a new continent*) Oklahoma City.

CORA (*Wearily*) I'll go out and fix supper, although I don't imagine any of us will feel like eating.

SONNY I do. I'm hungry.

CORA (*A little amused*) Are you? Good. Come to me, Sonny! (*With a sudden need for affection*) Do you love me, boy? Do you love your old mom?

SONNY More than all the world with a fence around it.

CORA (*Clasping him to her*) Oh, God, what would I do without you kids? I hope you'll always love me, Sonny. I hope you always will. (REENIE *comes downstairs*) Where are you going, daughter?
(REENIE *looks disdainfully at them, and marches into the parlor, where, in a moment, we hear her playing a lovely Chopin nocturne*)

SONNY Mom, I'm going to sell my autographed photograph of Fatty Arbuckle. Millicent Dalrymple said she'd give me fifteen cents for it. And Fatty Arbuckle isn't one of my favorites any more. If I sold the photograph, I'd have enough to go to the movie tonight and buy a sack of popcorn, besides.

CORA (*Lying on the floor beside him*) If the world was falling to pieces all about you, you'd still want to go to the movies, wouldn't you?

SONNY I don't see why not.

CORA Your mother's unhappy, Sonny. Doesn't that mean anything to you?

SONNY Well . . . I'm sorry.

CORA I want you kids near me tonight. Can't you understand? Oh, God, wouldn't it be nice if life were as sweet
as music! (*For a moment, mother and son lie together in
each other's arms. Then* CORA *stands, as though fearing
her own indulgence, and takes* SONNY *by the hand*) Come!
Help me set the table, Sonny.

CURTAIN

ACT TWO

Act Two

SCENE: *At rise of curtain, we hear a banging rendition of "Smiles" coming from the parlor, where* LOTTIE *is at the piano,* SONNY *by her side, both singing in hearty voices.* REENIE *stands listlessly watching, drying a dish.* MORRIS *sits in* RUBIN'S *chair, working one of those baffling little hand puzzles, which has got the best of him.* LOTTIE *proves to be a big, fleshy woman, a few years older than* CORA. *She wears a gaudy dress and lots of costume jewelry.* MORRIS *is a big defeated-looking man of wrecked virility.*

LOTTIE and SONNY (*Singing*)   "There are smiles that make us happy . . ."

CORA (*Coming into living room from kitchen*)   I won't need you to help me with the dishes, Reenie. I want you to go upstairs now and get ready for your party. (*Calls into parlor*) Sonny! Sonny!

MORRIS   Sure was a good dinner, Cora.

CORA   What, Morris?

MORRIS (*Trying to make himself heard above the piano*) I said, it sure was a good dinner.

CORA   Thank you, Morris. Now go and get dressed, Reenie. (REENIE *reluctantly goes upstairs*) Sonny! Sonny! Lottie, will you please stop that racket. A body can't hear himself think.
(LOTTIE *and* SONNY *finish the chorus*)

CORA   Sonny, I said you've got to help me in the kitchen.

SONNY   Why can't Reenie?

CORA   She cleared the table for me, and now she has to bathe and get ready for her party.

SONNY   I have to do everything around here.

39

LOTTIE (*In the voice one uses to indulge a child*)   I think it's a shame. (SONNY *and* CORA *exit into the dining room.* LOTTIE *comes into the living room. To* MORRIS) Cora always was jealous because I could play the piano and she couldn't. (*Looks to see if* CORA *is out of hearing distance*) Do I have something to tell you! Do you know why she asked us over here?
(*She hurries over to* MORRIS)

MORRIS   For dinner.

LOTTIE   No! She and Rubin have had another fight. She told me all about it while I was in the kitchen helping her get dinner on the table.

MORRIS   What about, this time?

LOTTIE   About a new dress she bought for Reenie. But what difference does that make? They could fight about anything. Only this time he hit her.

MORRIS   He did?

LOTTIE   Don't tell her I told you. Poor Cora. I guess maybe she has a hard time with Rubin.

MORRIS   Has Rubin walked out again?

LOTTIE   You guessed it. Do you know what she wants to do now, honey? She wants to bring the kids over to Oklahoma City to live *with us?* She says I suggested they do that some time ago. I guess maybe I did, but my God, I never thought they'd do it. We'd be perfectly miserable with her and the two kids living with us, wouldn't we, Morris? With only one extra bedroom, one of 'em would have to sleep on the davenport in the living room, and then what would happen when your patients started coming in the morning?

MORRIS   Yah. It wouldn't work out very well.

LOTTIE   No. Oh, my! The way she pampers those kids, Morris. If she had her way, she'd spoil 'em rotten.

MORRIS   What did you tell her, honey?

LOTTIE   Well, I haven't told her anything yet. I was so
flabbergasted when she asked me, I just hemmed . . .
(SONNY *enters the parlor to put away a big vase that*
CORA *has just washed.* LOTTIE *sees him*)   Hi! Honey.

SONNY   They got me working again.

LOTTIE   I think it's terrible.
(SONNY *exits into the dining room*)

LOTTIE   . . . and hawed until I could think of something to
say. Oh, Morris, put away that puzzle and listen to me.
She's going to come to you sometime this evening and ask
you about it, and all you need to say is, "I'm leaving all
that in Lottie's hands, Cora." Can you remember that?
Just say it real nice, like it was none of your business.

MORRIS   I'll remember.

LOTTIE   You say you will, but will you?

MORRIS   Yes, honey.

LOTTIE   I don't know. You're so afraid of hurting people's
feelings.

MORRIS   That's not so.

LOTTIE   Oh, it is too. Don't I know! You had to go to see
some psychologist over in Oklahoma City because you
were so afraid of hurting your patients when you drilled
their teeth. Now, confess it. It was actually making you
sick, that you had to drill your patients' teeth and hurt
them.

MORRIS   Honey, I wasn't really *sick* about it.

LOTTIE   You were too. Now remember what I say. Don't
get *soft-hearted* at the last minute and tell Cora to bring
the kids and come on over. My God, Morris, we'd be in
the loony bin in less than two days with them in the

house. Cora may be my own flesh and blood but I couldn't live with her to save my life. And I love those kids of hers. I do, Morris. But I couldn't live with them. They'd drive me crazy. You, too. You know they would.

CORA (*Enters the parlor to put napkins in the sideboard*) Almost finished.

LOTTIE   You shoulda let me help you. (*But* CORA *has returned to the kitchen*) Cora said something to me about her getting a job at one of the big department stores over in Oklahoma City. Can you see her doin' a thing like that? I can't. "Cora," I said, "you wouldn't last two days at that kind of work, on your feet all day, taking people's sass." Well, I don't know if I convinced her or not, but I gave her something to think about. (*Sneaks back to parlor door to see if* CORA *is within earshot, then comes back to* MORRIS, *speaking in a very confidential voice*) Morris? Do you think Rubin still plays around with Mavis Pruitt over in Ponca City?

MORRIS (*Clamming up*)   I don't know, honey.

LOTTIE   You do too.

MORRIS   I'm telling you, I don't.

LOTTIE   You men, you tell each other everything, but you all want to protect each other. And wild horses and screaming ravens couldn't get you to talk.

MORRIS   Well, whatever Rubin does . . . like that . . . is *his* business.

LOTTIE   My! Don't we sound righteous all of a sudden! Well, I bet anything he still sees her.

MORRIS   Well, don't you let on to Cora.

LOTTIE   I won't. Did I ever tell you about the first time she met Rubin?

MORRIS   Yes, honey.

LOTTIE   I did not! Cora and I were coming out of the five-and-ten. She'd wanted to buy a little lace to put on a dress. And here comes Rubin, like a picture of Sin, riding down the street on a shiny black horse. My God, he was handsome. Neither of us knew who he was. But he looked at Cora and smiled, and Cora began to get all nervous and fluttery. And do you know what? He came by the house that very night and wanted to see her. Mama and Papa didn't know what to do. They stood around like they were afraid of Rubin. But Cora went out riding with him. He'd brought a buggy with him. And six weeks later they were married. Mama and Papa were worried sick. Rubin's people were all right, but they were ranchers. Kind of wild. And Cora only seventeen, not out of high school. I think that's the reason Papa had his stroke, don't you, Morris?

MORRIS   Maybe . . .

LOTTIE   I do. They just felt like Cora might as well be dead as married to a man like Rubin. But Cora was always a determined creature. Mama and Papa were no match for her when she wanted her own way.

MORRIS   Well, I like Rubin.

LOTTIE   I do, too, honey. I'm not saying anything against him. And he's made a lot better husband than I ever thought he would. But I'm glad *I'm* not married to him. I'd be worried to death all the time. I'm glad I'm married to a nice man I can trust.
(MORRIS *does not know how to respond to this endearment. He crosses the room troubledly*)

MORRIS   What'll Cora do if Rubin doesn't come back?

LOTTIE   Well, that's not our problem, honey.

MORRIS   Yes, but just the same, I . . .

LOTTIE   Listen, she's got a nice big house here, hasn't she? She can take in roomers if she has to. And Mama left her two thousand dollars when she died, didn't she? Yes, Cora was the baby, so Mama left the money to her. I'm not going to worry.

REENIE (*Upstairs*)   Aunt Lottie!

MORRIS   All right. I was just wondering.

LOTTIE   Now, remember. All you've got to say is, "I'm leaving all that to Lottie, Cora."

MORRIS   Yes, honey.
(REENIE *comes downstairs looking somewhat wan and frightened*)

LOTTIE   Shhhh! (*Now she turns to* REENIE *with a prepared smile*) Well, honey, aren't you getting ready for your party? Morris and I are dying to see your new dress.

RENNIE   I don't feel well. I wish I didn't have to go.

LOTTIE (*Alarmed*)   You don't feel well? Did you tell your mother?

REENIE   Yes. But she won't believe me. I wish you'd tell her, Aunt Lottie.

LOTTIE (*Rushes excitedly into dining room, where we hear her speaking to* CORA)   Cora! Reenie says she isn't feeling well. Cora, I think maybe she shouldn't go to the party. She says she doesn't want to go. Cora, what do you think is wrong?

CORA (*Enters living room from dining room—followed by* LOTTIE)   There's nothing wrong with the child, Lottie.

LOTTIE   But she says she isn't feeling well, Cora. (*Turns to* REENIE) Come here, honey, let me see if you've got a temperature. No. Not a sign of temperature. Stick out your tongue. Are you sick at your stomach?

REENIE   Kind of.

LOTTIE   My God, Cora. Her little hands are like ice.

CORA (*Quite calm and wise*) There's nothing wrong with the child, Lottie. She gets to feeling like this every time she goes to a party.

LOTTIE She's not going to have a very good time if she doesn't feel well.

CORA It's something she's got to get over, Lottie. Plans are already made now. I got her the dress and she's got a date with a boy who's come here all the way from California. Now, I'm not going to let her play sick and not go. The Ralston girl would never invite Reenie to another party as long as she lived if she backed out now.
(*Her strategy defeated,* REENIE *goes back up the stairs*)

LOTTIE It's awful funny when a young girl doesn't want to go to a party, don't you think so, Morris? (*She watches* REENIE'S *departure, puzzledly*) I just thought of something. I've got a bottle of perfume I'm going to give her. It's Coty's L'Origan. Finest perfume made. One of the big drugstores in Oklahoma City was having an anniversary sale. With each box of Coty's face powder, they gave you a little bottle of perfume, stuck right on top of the box. Morris, run out to the car and get me that package. It's on the back seat. I'll take it upstairs to Reenie. It'll make her feel good, don't you think?

CORA That's very thoughtful of you, Lottie.

MORRIS (*On his way to door*) You'll have her smelling like a fancy woman.

LOTTIE (*With a sudden bite*) How do *you* know what a fancy woman smells like?

MORRIS I can make a joke, can't I?
(MORRIS *exits.* CORA *and* LOTTIE *sit on either side of the table*)

LOTTIE It was a wonderful dinner, Cora.

CORA I'm glad you thought so. It all tasted like ashes to me.

LOTTIE   Oh, now, Cora, quit taking on.

CORA   Seventeen years we've been married, Lottie, and we still can't get along.

LOTTIE   What are you talking about? Why, I've known times when you got along just fine . . . for months at a time.

CORA   When Rubin was gone.

LOTTIE   Cora, that's not so.

CORA   Lottie, it's not good for kids to see their parents fighting.

LOTTIE   Cora, you've got the two nicest kids in the whole world. Why, they're wonderful children, Cora.

CORA   I worry about them, Lottie . . . You saw Reenie just now. Here she is, sick because she's going to a party, when most girls her age would be tickled to death. And the other boys tease Sonny so.

LOTTIE   Oh, Reenie'll get over that. So will Sonny.

CORA   Kids don't just "get over" these things, in some magic way. These troubles stay with kids sometimes, and affect their lives when they grow up.

MORRIS   (*Returns with a small package*)   This what you want?

LOTTIE   Yes. Reenie—I've got something for you, Reenie. I've got something here to make you smell good. Real French perfume. Morris says it'll make you smell like a fancy woman.
(*She goes running upstairs, exuding her own brand of warmth and affection*)

CORA   Lottie's awful good-hearted, Morris.

MORRIS   She thinks an awful lot of your kids, Cora.

CORA   I know she does. Morris, I've been thinking, wouldn't it be nice if Sonny and Reenie could go to those big schools you have in Oklahoma City? I mean . . .

LOTTIE   (*Hurrying back downstairs*)   Cora, I wish you'd let me curl Reenie's hair for her. I could have her looking like a real baby doll. I'm an artist at it. Last week, Morris took me to a party at the Shrine, and everybody told me I had the prettiest head of hair at the whole party.

CORA   Go on and do it.

LOTTIE   I can't right now. She's in the bathtub. When are you going to get your hair bobbed, Cora?

CORA   Rubin doesn't like bobbed hair.

LOTTIE   Oh, he doesn't! You like my bobbed hair, don't you, Morris?

MORRIS   It's all right, honey.

LOTTIE   I'll be darned if I'd let any man tell me whether I could bob my hair or not. Why, I wouldn't go back to long hair now for anything. Morris says maybe I should take up smoking cigarettes now. Would you believe it, Cora? Women all over Oklahoma City are smoking cigarettes now. Isn't that disgraceful? What in God's name are we all coming to?

CORA   (*There is too much on her mind for her to partake now of* LOTTIE'S *small talk*)   I . . . I'd better finish up in the kitchen.
(*She exits through the dining-room door*)

LOTTIE   Morris, I don't know what to do. I just can't bear to see little Cora so unhappy.

MORRIS   After all, it's not your worry, honey.

LOTTIE   Oh, I know, but in a way it *is* my worry. I mean, I've always looked after Cora, ever since we were girls. I took her to her teacher the first day of school. I gave up the wishbone for her every time we had fried chicken. She was the baby of the family, and I guess we all felt we had to pamper her.

MORRIS   Honey, if you want to take in her and the kids, it's up to you. We'd manage somehow.

LOTTIE   Oh, God, Morris! Life'd be miserable.

SONNY (*Enters through parlor*)   Wanta see my movie stars, Aunt Lottie?

LOTTIE   I guess so, honey. (SONNY *goes into parlor to get scrapbooks as* LOTTIE *turns to* MORRIS *with a private voice*) Every time we come over here we've got to look at his movie stars.

MORRIS   Got any of Norma Talmadge?

SONNY (*Spreading the scrapbook on the floor before them*) Sure.

LOTTIE   Norma Talmadge, Norma Talmadge! That's all you ever think about is Norma Talmadge. I don't know what you see in her. Besides, she's a Catholic.

MORRIS   Honey, you've just got a bug about the Catholics.

LOTTIE   Oh I do, do I! Maybe you'd like to marry Norma Talmadge someday and then let the Pope tell you what to do the rest of your life, making you swear to leave all your money to the church, and bring up all your children Catholic, and then join the Knights of Columbus and take an oath to go out and kill all the nice Protestant women when the day comes for the Catholics to take over the world.
(CORA *enters the parlor on her way to the sideboard, then wanders into the living room*)

MORRIS   Honey, where do you pick up these stories?

LOTTIE   Well, it's the truth. Marietta Flagmeyer told me. Cora, Marietta has this very close friend who used to be a

Catholic but isn't any more. She even joined a convent, but she ran away because she found out all those things and wouldn't stand for them. This friend told Marietta that the Catholics keep the basements of their churches filled with guns and all kinds of ammunition . . .

CORA (*She has heard* LOTTIE'S *rantings before*) Lottie! (*She shakes her head hopelessly and returns to the parlor, on her way to the kitchen*)

LOTTIE . . . because some day they plan to rise and take over the world, and kill off all the rest of us who don't want to be Catholics. I believe every word of it, too.

MORRIS Well . . . I still like Norma Talmadge. Got any of Bebe Daniels?

SONNY Yes. (*He hands* MORRIS *a picture, which* LOTTIE *snaps up first for an approving look*)

LOTTIE I don't know what you see in her. (*She now passes the picture on to* MORRIS)

MORRIS You don't like any of the women stars, honey.

LOTTIE I guess I don't. I hear they're all a bunch of trollops. (*To* SONNY) Honey, when is your daddy coming home?

SONNY Oh, he's not coming back at all. He and Mom had a fight. Here's one of your favorites, Aunt Lottie. (*He hands her a picture*)

LOTTIE Who? Rudolph Valentino. He's not one of my favorites at all.

MORRIS You saw *The Sheik* four times.

LOTTIE That's just because Marietta Flagmeyer wanted me to keep her company.

MORRIS Rudolph Valentino must be a Catholic, too. He's an Eyetalian.

LOTTIE But he's not a Catholic. Marietta's friend has a book that lists all the people in Hollywood who are Catholics. (*She studies the picture very intently*) You know, it scares me a little to look at him. Those eyes, that seem to be laughing at you, and all those white teeth. I think it's a sin for a man to be as pretty as he is. Why, I'd be scared to death to let a man like him touch me. (CORA *returns now, without her apron; she is carrying a paper bag*) But you know, they say he's really a very nice man. Cora, do you know there's this woman over in Oklahoma City who worships Rudolph Valentino? That's the truth. Marietta knows her. She's made a little shrine to him down in her basement, and she keeps the room filled with candles and she goes down there every day and says a little prayer for him.

CORA I thought you were going to fix Reenie's hair.

LOTTIE Oh, yes. I guess she's out of the bathtub now.

CORA (*Puts the bag on the table*) There's a lot of fried chicken left, Lottie. I brought you some to take home with you.

LOTTIE Won't you and the kids want it?

CORA They won't eat anything but the breast.

LOTTIE Thanks, Cora.

CORA Sonny, I don't want your pictures all over the floor when the young people come by for Reenie.

SONNY All right.

MORRIS (*As* LOTTIE *takes a drumstick out of the bag*) Honey, you just ate.

LOTTIE Don't scold me, Daddy. (*She whispers boldly to him before starting upstairs*) Remember what I told you, Morris. (*Now she goes hurrying up the stairs*) Reenie! I'm coming up to fix your hair. I'm going to turn you into a real baby doll.

REENIE (*Upstairs*) I'm in here, Aunt Lottie.
(MORRIS *draws over to the door, as though hoping to evade*
CORA)

CORA Morris . . . Morris! I suppose Lottie told you what's
happened.

MORRIS Well, uh . . . yes, Cora . . . she said something
about it.

CORA I guess now that maybe my folks were right, Morris. I
shouldn't have married Rubin.

MORRIS You're going to forget all this squabble after a
while, Cora. So's Rubin.

CORA I don't think we *should* forget it. I don't think we
should *try* to come back together. I think I've failed.

MORRIS Now, Cora, I think you're exaggerating things in
your own mind.

CORA Morris, I'm only thirty-four. That's still young. I
thought I'd like to take the kids to Oklahoma City and put
them in school there, and get myself a job in one of the department stores. I know I've never done work like that, but
I think I'd like it, and . . . it seems to me that I've got to,
Morris. I've got to.

MORRIS Well, Cora . . . maybe . . .

LOTTIE (*Upstairs we see her feet treading the hallway*) Let's
go into the bathroom, Reenie, where the light's better.

MORRIS It's awful hard, Cora, being on your feet all day.

CORA But I'd get used to it.

MORRIS Well . . . it's hard for me to advise you, Cora.

CORA Morris, I was wondering if maybe the kids and I could
come and live with you and Lottie for a while. Just for a

while. Until we got used to the city. Until I got myself a job and we felt more or less at home.

MORRIS   Well, I . . . uh . . .

CORA   I promise we wouldn't be any bother. I mean, I'd keep things straightened up after the kids, and do as much of the cooking as Lottie wanted me to do.

MORRIS   Well, I . . . uh . . .

CORA   I just don't know what else the kids and I can do, Morris.

MORRIS   Yes. Well . . . Cora, I don't know just what to say.

CORA   Would we be too much in the way, Morris?

MORRIS   Oh, no. Of course not, Cora. *But . . .*

CORA   (*Hopefully*)   I think we could manage. And I'd pay our share of the bills. I'd insist on that.
(FLIRT, PUNKY *and* SAMMY *are seen through the window, coming onto the porch*)

MORRIS   Well, Cora, I . . .

LOTTIE   (*Comes hurtling halfway down the stairs, full of anxiety*)   Cora, Reenie's sick. She's vomiting all over the bathroom.
(*She bustles back upstairs as* CORA *starts to follow*)

CORA   Oh, my God! (*The doorbell rings, catching* CORA *for a moment*) Oh, dear! It's the young people after Reenie. Sonny, put on your manners and answer the door. (SONNY *runs to the door, stopping to turn on the porch light before opening it. We see the three young people on the porch outside—*FLIRT *in dazzling party dress, and the two boys in uniforms from a nearby military academy. One boy,* PUNKY GIVENS, *is seen drinking from a flask, preparing himself to meet people. Inside,* CORA *starts upstairs in worried concern*) Oh, dear! What could be wrong with the child! Morris, try to entertain the young people until I get back.

(CORA *goes off*. SONNY *swings open the door*)

SONNY   Won't you come in?

FLIRT   (*Comes dancing into the hallway, bringing the atmosphere of a chilly spring night with her*) Hi, Sonny! Is your sister ready?

SONNY   Not yet.

FLIRT   Oh, shucks! (*Sticks her head out the door*) Come on in, fellows. We're going to have to wait. (PUNKY GIVENS *and* SAMMY GOLDENBAUM *make a colorful entrance. Both are dressed in uniforms of lustrous blue, which fit them like smooth upholstery.* FLIRT *begins the introductions*) Sammy, this is Sonny Flood, Reenie's little brother.

(SAMMY GOLDENBAUM *steps forth correctly, his plumed headgear in his hand. He is a darkly beautiful young man of seventeen, with lustrous black hair, black eyes and a captivating smile. Yet, something about him seems a little foreign, at least in comparison with the Midwestern company in which he now finds himself. He could be a Persian prince, strayed from his native kingdom. But he has become adept over the years in adapting himself, and he shows an eagerness to make friends and to be liked*)

SAMMY   Hi, Sonny!

SONNY   (*Shaking hands*)   Hi!

FLIRT   (*Bringing* PUNKY *up from the rear*)   And this is Punky Givens. (*She all but drags him from the dark corner of the hallway to face the lighted room full of people. For* PUNKY *is a disappointment as a human being. The military academy has done nothing as yet for his posture, and he wears his uniform as though embarrassed by its splendor. He offers a limp hand when being introduced, mumbles some incoherent greeting, and then retires in hopes that no one will notice him. These introductions made,* FLIRT *now notices* MORRIS) Oh, hello! I'm Flirt Conroy. How're you?

MORRIS   How d'ya do? I'm Morris Lacey. Reenie's uncle. From Oklahoma City.

FLIRT   Oh, yes, I've heard her speak about you. Fellows, this is Dr. Lacey. He's Reenie's uncle. From Oklahoma City.

SAMMY (*Crossing the room to present himself to* MORRIS, *he is brisk and alert, even though his speech betrays a slight stammer*)   How do you do, sir? My name is G-Goldenbaum. Sammy, they call me.

MORRIS   Glad to know you, Sammy.

FLIRT   And this is Punky Givens. (*Nudging him*) Stand up straight, Punky.

MORRIS   Glad to know you, Punky. (PUNKY *mumbles.* MORRIS *now feels the burden of his responsibility as temporary host*) Uh . . . anyone care for a Life Saver? (*He offers a pack from his pocket, but no one is interested.* LOTTIE *comes bustling down the stairs, eager to take over the situation, exuberantly babbling inconsequentials all the way down*)

LOTTIE   Hello, everyone! I'm Lottie Lacey, Reenie's aunt. I'm Cora Flood's sister. From Oklahoma City. Oklahoma City's a great big town now. People say in another ten years it's going to be the biggest city in the whole United States, bigger even than New York or Chicago. You're the little Conroy girl, aren't you? I've heard my sister speak of you. My! What a pretty red dress. Have you all met my husband? Dr. Lacey. He's a dentist. Come over to Oklahoma City and he'll pull all your teeth. (*She laughs heartily, and then her eyes slowly widen at the magnificent uniforms*) My goodness! Aren't those handsome getups?

SAMMY (*Stepping forth*)   How do you do, ma'am? I'm Sammy Goldenbaum. From California.

LOTTIE   Oh, yes. Cora told me about the young man from California. He's from Hollywood, Morris. His mother's in the movies. Has she played in anything I might have seen?

SAMMY   She was in T-Thomas Meighan's last picture. Her
name is Gertrude Vanderhof. It was a very small part. She
isn't a star or anything.

LOTTIE   Gertrude Vanderhof! Did we see Thomas Meighan's
last picture, Morris? I don't believe so. I like Thomas
Meighan, but we don't have time to see *all* the movies. Do
you think you ever saw Gertrude Vanderhof in anything,
Morris?
(LOTTIE *seems to refer to her husband on every topic without waiting for his judgment. Nevertheless,* MORRIS *mulls
over this last query as* FLIRT *interrupts*)

FLIRT   Mrs. Lacey, have you met Punky Givens?

LOTTIE   How do you do? I've heard my sister speak of you.
Your people are very prominent in town, aren't they? Yes,
I've heard Cora speak of them. (PUNKY *offers a hand and
mumbles*) What did you say? (*He repeats his mumble.*
LOTTIE *is still at sea but makes the best of things*) Thank
you very much.
(*At the top of the stairs, we see* REENIE'S *feet trying to
get up the courage to bring her down, and we hear* CORA
coaxing her)

CORA   (*Off*)   Go on, Reenie.
(*But* REENIE *can't make it yet. The feet go scurrying back
to safety*)

LOTTIE   (*Trying to avoid embarrassment*)   Well, I'm afraid
you're all going to have to wait a few minutes. Reenie isn't
quite ready.

CORA   (*Upstairs*)   Reenie, not another word.

LOTTIE   Cora's upstairs now, helping her. I guess you'll have
to entertain yourselves a while. Do any of you play mah-
jong?
(*She notices the bag of fried chicken, and hides it under
the table*)

FLIRT   I want to play some music. Got any new piano rolls,
Sonny?

SONNY   A few.
  (*They run into the parlor, to the piano*)

FLIRT   Gee, I wish you had a Victrola like we do.

LOTTIE (*Sitting, turning her attention to* SAMMY) My,
  you're a long way from home, aren't you?

SAMMY   Yes, ma'am.

LOTTIE   Morris and I went to California once. A Shriners'
  convention. Oh, we thought it was perfectly wonderful, all
  those oranges and things. Didn't we, Morris? I should think
  you'd want to go home on your spring vacation.

SAMMY   Well, I . . . I guess I don't really have a home
  . . . Mrs. Lacey.
  (SONNY *wanders back from the parlor.* SAMMY *fills him
  with curiosity and fascination*)

LOTTIE   Did you tell me your mother lived out there?

SAMMY   Yes, but, you see, she's pretty busy in moving pictures, and . . . Oh, she feels awfully bad that she doesn't
  have more time for me. Really she does. But she doesn't
  have a place where I could stay right now . . . and . . .
  But, it's not *her* fault.

LOTTIE   Where's your father?

SAMMY   Oh, I never knew him.

LOTTIE   You never knew your father?

SAMMY   No. You see, he died before I was born. My mother
  has been married . . . a few times since then. But I never
  met any of her husbands . . . although they were all very
  fine gentlemen.

LOTTIE   Well—I just never knew anyone who didn't have a
  home. Do you spend your whole life in military academies?

SAMMY   Just about. I bet I've been in almost every military academy in the whole country. Well, I take that back. There's some I didn't go to. I mean . . . there's some that wouldn't take me.

SONNY (*Out of the innocent blue*) My mother says you're a Jew.

LOTTIE (*Aghast*) Sonny!

SAMMY Well . . . yes, Sonny. I guess I am.

LOTTIE (*Consolingly*) That's perfectly all right. Why, we don't think a thing about a person's being Jewish, do we, Morris?

MORRIS No. Of course not.

SAMMY My father was Jewish. Mother told me. Mother isn't Jewish at all. Oh, my mother has the most beautiful blond hair. I guess I take after my father . . . in looks, anyhow. He was an actor, too, but he got killed in an automobile accident.

LOTTIE That's too bad. Sonny, I think you should apologize.

SONNY Did I say something bad?

SAMMY Oh, that's all right. It doesn't bother me that I'm Jewish. Not any more. I guess it used to a little . . . Yes, it did used to a little.

LOTTIE (*Who must find a remedy for everything*) You know what you ought to do? You ought to join the Christian Science church. Now, I'm not a member myself, but I know this Jewish woman over in Oklahoma City, and she was very, very unhappy, wasn't she, Morris? But she joined the Christian Science church and has been perfectly happy ever since.

SONNY I didn't mean to say anything wrong.

SAMMY You didn't say anything wrong, Sonny.

(*The piano begins playing "The Sheik of Araby" with precise, automatic rhythm.* FLIRT *dances in from the parlor*)

FLIRT   Come on, Punky, let's dance. (*She sings*) The Shiek of Araby—boom—boom—boom—his heart belongs to me. Come *on*, Punky.

SAMMY (*Always courteous, to* LOTTIE)   Would you care to dance, ma'am?

LOTTIE   Me? Good heavens, no. I haven't danced since I was a girl. But I certainly appreciate your asking. Isn't he respectful, Morris?
(LOTTIE *exits to dining room*)

SAMMY   Wanta wild West ride, Sonny?
(*He kneels on the floor, permitting* SONNY *to straddle his back. Then* SAMMY *kicks his feet in the air like a wild colt, as* SONNY *holds to him tight*)

FLIRT (*At the back of the room, instructs* PUNKY *in the intricacies of a new step*)   No, Punky. That's not it. You take one step to the left and then *dip*. See? Oh, it's a wonderful step, and all the kids are doing it.

LOTTIE (*Enters from kitchen with a plate of cookies, which she offers to* SAMMY *and* SONNY)   Would you like a cookie?

SAMMY (*Getting to his feet, the ride over*)   Gee, that gets to be pretty strenuous.
(FLIRT *and* PUNKY *now retire to the parlor where they indulge in a little private lovemaking*)

SONNY   Where did you get those clothes?

SAMMY   They gave them to me at the academy, Sonny.

FLIRT (*Protesting* PUNKY'S *advances*)   Punky, *don't*.
(LOTTIE *observes this little intimacy, having just started into the parlor with the plate of cookies. It rouses some of her righteousness*)

SAMMY   No. I take that back. They didn't *give* them to me.
They never give you anything at that place. I paid for them.
Plenty!

SONNY   Why do you wear a sword?

SAMMY   (*Pulls the sword from its sheath, like a buccaneer,
and goes charging about the room in search of imagined
villains*)   I wear a sword to protect myself! See! To kill
off all the villains in the world. (*He frightens* LOTTIE)   Oh,
don't worry, ma'am. It's not sharp. I couldn't hurt anyone
with it, even if I wanted so. We just wear them for show.

SONNY   (*Jumping up and down*)   Can I have a sword? I
want a sword.

SAMMY   Do you, Sonny? Do you want a sword? Here,
Sonny, I'll give you *my* sword, for all the good it'll do you.

LOTTIE   (*To* MORRIS)   Cora will probably buy Sonny a
sword now. (*Now* SONNY *takes the sword and imitates the
actions of* SAMMY. LOTTIE *is apprehensive*)   Now, you be
careful, Sonny.

SAMMY   What do you want a sword for, Sonny?

SONNY   (*With a lunge*)   To *show* people.

LOTTIE   Sonny! Be careful with that thing.

SAMMY   And what do you want to show people, Sonny?

SONNY   I just want to *show* 'em.
(*He places the sword between his arm and his chest, then
drops to the floor, the sword rising far above his body, giving the appearance that he is impaled.* LOTTIE *is horrified*)

LOTTIE   Oh, darling—put it down. Sonny, please don't play
with that nasty thing any more.
(SONNY *rises now and laughs with* SAMMY. LOTTIE *puts
the sword away in the parlor, where she again comes upon*
FLIRT *and* PUNKY, *now engaged in more serious necking.
Morally outraged, she runs up the stairs to inform* CORA)

SAMMY (*Kneeling beside* SONNY, *as though to make himself a physical equal*)   What'll we do now, Sonny? Are there any games you want to play? Do you want to fight Indians? or set bear traps? or go flying over volcanoes? or climb the Alps?

SONNY (*Eagerly*)   Yes . . . yes.

SAMMY   Gee, so do I, Sonny. But we can't. Not tonight anyway. What else can we do?

SONNY   I can show you my movie stars.

SAMMY   I've had enough of movie stars. What else?

SONNY   I can speak a piece.

SAMMY   You can? (*jumps to his feet*) Hey, everyone! Stop the music. Sonny's going to speak a piece.
(SAMMY *stops the piano, which* FLIRT *finds quite annoying*)

LOTTIE (*Hurrying downstairs*)   Did you hear that, Morris? Sonny's going to speak a piece.

FLIRT (*To* SAMMY)   Hey, what are you doing?

SAMMY (*To* SONNY)   Where do you want to stand, sir?

LOTTIE   He's got a little platform in the parlor where he practices.

SAMMY (*Having taken over as impresario*)   Into the parlor, everyone. Into the parlor to hear Sonny speak his piece.

FLIRT (*Pulling* PUNKY'S *arm*)   Come on, Punky. Come on. We *have* to listen, don't we?

SAMMY   Quiet, everyone. Quiet!
(*All enter the parlor, except* MORRIS, *who crosses toward the door, as though he hoped to escape, as* SONNY *begins the famous soliloquy with boyish fervor.* MORRIS *looks as*

though he might share some of Hamlet's woes. After
SONNY *begins,* CORA *starts down the stairs with* REENIE.)

SONNY
   "To be, or not to be: that is the question:
   Whether 'tis nobler in the mind to suffer
   The slings and arrows of outrageous fortune,
   Or to take arms against a sea of troubles,
   And by opposing end them? To die: to sleep;
   No more; and, by a sleep to say we end
   The heart-ache and the thousand natural shocks
   That flesh is heir to, 'tis a consummation
   Devoutly to be wish'd. To die, to sleep;
   To sleep; perchance to dream: ay, there's the rub,
   For in that sleep of death what dreams may come
   When we have shuffled off this mortal coil,
   Must give us pause. . . ."

CORA   (*While* SONNY *is reciting*)   Oh, Sonny's reciting. Why,
   he's reciting Shakespeare. He must have gotten out that
   dusty volume of Shakespeare over in the bookcase, and
   memorized that speech all on his own. (*Points to* SAMMY
   in the parlor) Reenie, there's your young man. Isn't he
   handsome? Now you're going to have a good time. I can
   feel it in my bones.
   (SONNY *and* CORA *finish speaking at the same time. There
   is immediate loud acclaim for* SONNY)

SAMMY   That was *wonderful*, Sonny.
   (*All come into the living room now,* SAMMY *carrying*
   SONNY *on his shoulders like a triumphant hero*)

LOTTIE   He's a second Jackie Coogan.

FLIRT   That was just wonderful, Sonny.

LOTTIE   Cora, you should have been here. Sonny recited
   Shakespeare. It was just wonderful.

CORA   Yes. I heard him.

SAMMY   Sonny's a genius. I'm going to take you to Hollywood, Sonny, and put you in the movies. You'll be the greatest actor out there, Sonny.

FLIRT   Oh, I think Shakespeare's just wonderful. I'm going to read him sometime, really I am.

CORA (*Going to* SAMMY)   Good evening, young man. I'm Mrs. Flood.

SAMMY (*Putting* SONNY *down*)   Beg your pardon, ma'am. I'm Sonny Goldenbaum.

CORA   Welcome. I see my son's been entertaining you.

SAMMY   He sure has, ma'am.

CORA   He started speaking pieces about a year ago. Just picked it up. Some people think he's talented.

SAMMY   I think so, too, ma'am. Very.

CORA (*Brings* REENIE *forth*)   Reenie! Sammy, this is my daughter Reenie.

SAMMY   Good evening, Reenie.

REENIE (*Reluctantly*)   Good evening.

SAMMY   You certainly look nice. That's a very beautiful dress.

FLIRT   Isn't it cute! I helped her pick it out. (CORA *quietly grabs* FLIRT'S *arm and prevents her from taking over*) Ouch!

SAMMY   Gee! I didn't expect you to be . . . like you are. I mean . . . well, Punky told me you were a friend of Flirt's, so I just naturally thought you'd be . . . well, kind of like Flirt is. Although Flirt is a very nice girl. I didn't mean to imply anything against her. But . . . *you're* very nice, too, in a different way.

REENIE (*Still a little distrustful*)   Thank you . . .

SAMMY Would you call me *Sammy?*

REENIE Sammy.

SAMMY And may I call you Reenie?

REENIE I guess so.

SAMMY It's awfully nice of you to let me take you to the party. I know just how a girl feels, going out with some crazy guy she doesn't even know.

REENIE Oh . . . that's all right. After all, you don't know anything about me, either.

SAMMY You know, I've never been to many parties, have you?

REENIE Not many.

SAMMY I always worry that maybe people aren't going to like me, when I go to a party. Isn't that crazy? Do you ever get kind of a sick feeling in the pit of your stomach when you dread things? Gee, I wouldn't want to miss a party for anything. But every time I go to one, I have to reason with myself to keep from feeling that the whole world's against me. See, I've spent almost my whole life in military academies. My mother doesn't have a place for me, where she lives. She . . . she just doesn't know what else to do with me. But you mustn't misunderstand about my mother. She's really a very lovely person. I guess every boy thinks his mother is very beautiful, but my mother really is. She tells me in every letter she writes how sorry she is that we can't be together more, but she has to think of her work. One time we were together, though. She met me in San Francisco once, and we were together for two whole days. She let me take her to dinner and to a show and to dance. Just like we were sweethearts. It was the most wonderful time I ever had. And then I had to go back to the old military academy. Every time I walk into the barracks, I get kind of a depressed feeling. It's got hard stone walls. Pictures of generals hanging all over . . . oh, they're very fine gentlemen, but they all look so kind of hard-boiled and stern

. . . you know what I mean. (CORA *and* LOTTIE *stand together, listening to* SAMMY'S *speech with motherly expressions.* FLIRT *is bored.* PUNKY *is half asleep, and now he gives a sudden, audible yawn that startles everyone*) Well, gee! I guess I've bored you enough, telling you about myself.

CORA *and* LOTTIE   Oh, no. You haven't either.

FLIRT (*Impatient to get to the party*)   Come on, kids. Let's hurry.

SAMMY (*Tenderly, to* REENIE)   Are you ready?

CORA (*As though fearing* REENIE *might bolt and run*) Reenie?

REENIE   Yes.

SAMMY   May I help you into your wrap?
(*The word "wrap" is a false glorification of her Sunday coat, which he offers her, helping her into it*)

REENIE   Thank you.

CORA (*Whispering to* LOTTIE)   I wish I could have bought her one of those little fur jackets like Flirt is wearing.

FLIRT   Stand up straight, Punky, and say good night to everyone.
(PUNKY *tries again, but remains inarticulate*)

CORA (*Assuming that* PUNKY *said good night*)   Good night, Punky. Tell your mother hello for me.

FLIRT   Very pleased to have met you, Mr. and Mrs. Lacey. Good night, Mrs. Flood.

CORA   Good night, Flirt.

LOTTIE *and* MORRIS   Good night.

SONNY (*Pulling at* SAMMY'S *coat tails*) Do you have to go?

SAMMY I'm afraid I do, Sonny.

SONNY Can I go, too? Please? Can I go, too?

SAMMY Gee, I don't know. (*He thinks a moment and then consults* FLIRT *and* PUNKY) Hey, is there any reason Sonny can't come along? I promise to look after him. Think what a great time he'd have.
(FLIRT *and* PUNKY *look dubious*)

SONNY (*Takes his welcome immediately for granted and dances about the room joyously*) Goody, goody! I'm going to the party. I'm going to the party.

REENIE (*Running to* CORA'S *side*) Mother, I'm not going if Sonny goes too. Other girls don't have to be bothered by their little brothers.

CORA I agree with you, daughter.

FLIRT (*She loves to lash out when she has a victim*) No. It's not a kids' party, Sammy. That was a stupid idea. I think you should mind your own business.

CORA (*Trying to cool* FLIRT'S *temper*) Now, Flirt.

FLIRT (*To* REENIE) He's always trying to boss everyone.

CORA (*To* SAMMY) I guess Sonny'd better not go.

SONNY (*Crying, jumping in protest*) I want to go to the party. I want to go to the party.

SAMMY (*Trying to be consoling*) I guess it was a pretty dumb idea, Sonny.

SONNY I WANT TO GO TO THE PARTY! I WANT TO GO TO THE PARTY!
(SONNY *flies into a real tantrum now, throws himself on*

the floor, pounding the floor with his fists and kicking it with his toes, his face red with rage. CORA *and* LOTTIE *flutter about him like nervous hens)*

CORA   Sonny! Sonny! Stop it this instant. Sonny, I'll not let you go to another movie for a whole month if you don't stop.

LOTTIE   Oh, what'll I do? Oh, here, Sonny, do you want a little cookie, sweetheart?

FLIRT   Now we'll never get there.

CORA   I never can do a thing with him when he throws one of these tantrums.

SAMMY   (*Quietly goes to* SONNY'S *side and speaks in a voice that is firm with authority, yet still thoughtful and considerate*)   Sonny, that's no way to behave.

SONNY   (*Suddenly quiet*)   Isn't it?

SAMMY   No, Sonny. You mustn't ever act like that.

SONNY   (*More reasonable now*)   But I want to go to the party.

SAMMY   But if you act that way, no one's *ever* going to ask you to a party.

SONNY   Aren't they?

SAMMY   No, Sonny. You have to be a good boy before people ask you to parties. Even then, they don't always ask you.

SONNY   I love parties more than anything else in the world.

SAMMY   So do I, Sonny. I love parties, too. But there's lots of parties I can't go to.

SONNY   Honest?

SAMMY   Honest. It was wrong of me to suggest that you go to the party tonight. You're not old enough yet. You'll be old enough someday though, and then you can go to all the parties you like.

SONNY   Can I?

SAMMY   Sure. Now, I tell you what I'll do. I'll gather up all the favors I can find at the party. Want me to? And I'll give them to your sister to bring home to you. And then you can have a party here all by yourself. Would you like that? You can throw a big party in Sammy's honor, without any old grownups around to interfere. Will that make you happy?

SONNY   Yes, yes.

SAMMY   O.K. Are we still buddies?

SONNY   Yes.

SAMMY   Forever and ever?

SONNY   Forever and ever.
    (SONNY *impulsively hugs him*)

SAMMY   Gee! I love kids.

CORA   (*Awed as though by a miracle*) You're the first person in the entire world who's ever been able to do a thing with the boy when he goes into one of his tantrums.

SAMMY   You know, it's funny, but . . . I always seem to know just how kids feel.

FLIRT   (*Still impatient*) Come on, Sammy.
    (FLIRT and PUNKY *exit*)

CORA   Good night, Sammy. I hope you'll be able to come back sometime.

SAMMY   Thank you, ma'am. It's very nice to feel welcome.

LOTTIE *and* MORRIS   Good night. Come over to see us some-time in Oklahoma City. It's a big town. You can stay in the extra bedroom. I hope you like cats.

CORA   (*While* LOTTIE *and* MORRIS *are speaking*)   Oh, Reenie, don't forget your present. You're feeling better now, aren't you?

REENIE   Yes, Mom.

SAMMY   (*Breaking away from* LOTTIE *and* MORRIS)   Excuse me.
(SAMMY *offers* REENIE *his arm now, and together they walk proudly out*)

CORA   (*After they exit*)   Why, that's the nicest young man I ever met.

LOTTIE   I thought so, too, Cora. And my goodness, he was handsome. Morris says he felt sorry for him, though.

CORA   Sorry? Oh, Morris.

LOTTIE   He seemed like a perfectly happy boy to me. But Morris says he looked like a very unhappy boy to him. What makes you think that, Morris?

MORRIS   Oh . . . I don't know.

CORA   Unhappy? Why, he made himself right at home, didn't he?

LOTTIE   I should say he did. He was laughing and enjoying himself. But Morris says sometimes the people who act the happiest are really the saddest.

CORA   Oh, Morris.

LOTTIE   Morris, I think you make these things up. Ever since you went to that psychologist, you've gone around imagining everyone's unhappy. (MORRIS *quietly gets up and walks to the door, leaving* LOTTIE *to wonder if she has said anything wrong*)   Where are you going, Morris?

MORRIS   Thought I'd go out for a little walk, honey.
  (MORRIS *exits*)

LOTTIE   (*Following him to the door*)   Oh. Well, don't be
  gone long. We've got to get started back soon.

CORA   Oh, please don't talk about going.

LOTTIE   My God, Cora, we can't stay here all night. (*She
  peers out the window now, wondering about* MORRIS)
  Morris is funny, Cora. Sometimes he just gets up like that
  and walks away. I never know why. Sometimes he's gone
  for hours at a time. He says the walk helps his digestion,
  but I think it's because he just wants to get away from me
  at times. Did you ever notice how he is with people? Like
  tonight. He sat there when all the young people were here,
  and he didn't say hardly a word. His mind was a thousand
  miles away. Like he was thinking about something. He
  seems to be always thinking about something.

CORA   Morris is nice to you. You've got no right to com-
  plain.

LOTTIE   He's nice to me . . . in *some* ways.

CORA   Good heavens, Lottie! He gave you those red patent-
  leather slippers, and that fox neckpiece . . . you should
  be grateful.

LOTTIE   I know, but . . . there's *some* things he hasn't
  given me.

CORA   Lottie! That's not his fault. You've got no right to
  hold that against him!

LOTTIE   Oh, it's just fine for you to talk. You've got two nice
  kids to keep you company. What have I got but a house full
  of cats?

CORA   Lottie, you always claimed you never wanted children.

LOTTIE   Well . . . what else can I say to people?

CORA (*This is something of a revelation to her*) I just never knew.

LOTTIE (*Having suddenly decided to say it*) Cora . . . I can't let you and the kids come over and live with us.

CORA (*This is a blow to her*) Oh . . . Lottie.

LOTTIE I'm sorry, Cora. I just can't do it.

CORA Lottie, I was depending on you . . .

LOTTIE Maybe you've depended on me too much. Ever since you were a baby, you've run to me with your problems, and now I've got problems of my own.

CORA What am I going to do, Lottie?

LOTTIE Call up Rubin and ask him to come back. Beg him to come back, if you have to get down on your knees.

CORA I mustn't do that, Lottie.

LOTTIE Why not?

CORA Because we just can't keep from fighting, Lottie. You know that. I just don't think it's right, our still going on that way.

LOTTIE Do you still love him?

CORA Oh . . . don't ask me, Lottie.

LOTTIE Do you?

CORA Oh . . . yes.

LOTTIE Cora, I don't think you should listen to the stories those old Werpel sisters tell you.

CORA He's as good as admitted it, Lottie.

LOTTIE   Well, Cora, I don't think it means he likes you any
the less, because he's seen Mavis Pruitt a few times.

CORA   No . . . I know he loves me.

LOTTIE   (*Asking very cautiously*)   Does he still want to be
intimate?

CORA   That's only animal, Lottie. I couldn't indulge myself
that way if I didn't feel he was being honorable.

LOTTIE   (*Breaks into a sudden raucous laugh*)   My God, a
big handsome buck like Rubin! Who cares if he's honorable?

CORA   (*A little shocked*)   Lottie!

LOTTIE   (*We see now a sudden lewdness in* LOTTIE *that has
not been discernible before*)   Cora, did you hear what the
old maid said to the burglar? You see, the burglar came
walking into her bedroom with this big, long billy club
and . . .

CORA   Lottie!

LOTTIE   (*Laughing so hard she can hardly finish the story*)
And the old maid . . . she was so green she didn't know
what was happening to her, she said . . .

CORA   Lottie! That's enough. That's enough.

LOTTIE   (*Shamed now*)   Shucks, Cora. I don't see what's
wrong in having a little fun just telling stories.

CORA   Sometimes you talk shamefully, Lottie, and when I
think of the way Mama and Papa brought us up . . .

LOTTIE   Oh, Mama and Papa, Mama and Papa! Maybe they
didn't know as much as we gave them credit for.

CORA   You're changed since you were a girl, Lottie.

LOTTIE   What if I am!

CORA   I never heard such talk.

LOTTIE   Well, that's all it is. It's only talk. Talk, talk, talk.

CORA   Lottie, are you sure you can't take us in?

LOTTIE   It'd mean the end of my marriage too, Cora. You don't understand Morris. He's always nice and quiet around people, so afraid of hurting people's feelings. But he's the most nervous man around the house you ever saw. He'd try to make the best of it if you and the kids came over, but he'd go to pieces. I know he would.

CORA   Honest?

LOTTIE   I'm not joking, Cora. My God, you're not the only one who has problems. Don't think that for a minute.

CORA   A few minutes ago, you said *you* had problems, Lottie . . .

LOTTIE   Problems enough.

CORA   Tell me, Lottie.

LOTTIE   Oh, why should I?

CORA   Doesn't Morris ever make love to you any more?

LOTTIE   (*It takes her several moments to admit it*)   . . . No. It's been over three years since he even touched me . . . that way.

CORA   (*Another revelation*)   Lottie!

LOTTIE   It's the God's truth, Cora.

CORA   Lottie! What's wrong?

LOTTIE   How do I know what's wrong? How does anyone ever know what's wrong with anyone else?

CORA   I mean . . . is there another woman?

LOTTIE   Not unless she visits him from the spirit world.
(*This releases her humor again and she is diverted by
another story*) Oh, say, Cora, did I tell you about this
woman over in Oklahoma City who's been holding séances?
Well, Marietta went to her and . . . (*But suddenly, again,
she loses her humor and makes another sad admission*) Oh,
no, there isn't another woman. Sometimes I wish there was.

CORA   Lottie, you don't mean that.

LOTTIE   How the hell do *you* know what I mean? He's
around the house all day long, now that he's got his dental
office in the dining room. Day and night, day and night.
Sometimes I get tired of looking at him.

CORA   Oh, Lottie . . . I'd always felt you and Morris were
so devoted to each other. I've always felt you had an almost
perfect marriage.

LOTTIE   Oh, we're still devoted, still call each other "honey,"
just like we did on our honeymoon.

CORA   But what happened? Something must have happened
to . . .

LOTTIE   Did you notice the way Morris got up out of his
chair suddenly and just walked away, with no explanation
at all? Well, something inside Morris did the same thing
several years ago. Something inside him just got up and
went for a walk, and never came back.

CORA   I . . . just don't understand.

LOTTIE   Sometimes I wonder if maybe I've been too bossy.
Could be. But then, I always supposed that Morris *liked* me
because I was bossy.

CORA   I always envied you, having a husband you could boss.

LOTTIE   Yes, I can boss Morris because he just isn't there any more to fight back. He doesn't care any more if I boss him or not.

CORA   Just the same, he never hit you.

LOTTIE   I wish he would.

CORA   Lottie!

LOTTIE   I do. I wish to God someone *loved* me enough to hit me. You and Rubin fight. Oh, God I'd like a good fight. Anything'd be better than this *nothing*. Morris and I go around always being so sweet to each other, but sometimes I wonder maybe he'd like to kill me.

CORA   Lottie, you don't mean it.

LOTTIE   Do you remember how Mama and Papa used to caution us about men, Cora?

CORA   Yes, I remember.

LOTTIE   My God, they had me so afraid of ever giving in to a man, I was petrified.

CORA   So was I.

LOTTIE   Yes, you were until Rubin came along and practically raped you.

CORA   Lottie! I don't want Sonny to hear talk like that.

LOTTIE   Why not? Let him hear!

CORA   (*Newly aghast at her sister's boldness*) Lottie!

LOTTIE   Why do we feel we always have to protect kids?

CORA   Keep your voice down. Rubin never did anything like that.

LOTTIE   Didn't he?

CORA   Of course not!

LOTTIE   My God, Cora, he had you pregnant inside of two weeks after he started seeing you.

CORA   Sssh.

LOTTIE   I never told. I never even told Morris. My God, do you remember how Mama and Papa carried on when they found out?

CORA   I remember.

LOTTIE   And Papa had his stroke just a month after you were married. Oh, I thought Rubin was the wickedest man alive.

CORA   I never blamed Rubin for that. I was crazy in love with him. He just swept me off my feet and made all my objections seem kinda silly. He even made Mama and Papa seem silly.

LOTTIE   Maybe I shoulda married a man like that. I don't know. Maybe it was as much my fault as Morris'. Maybe I didn't . . . respond right . . . from the very first.

CORA   What do you mean, Lottie?

LOTTIE   Cora, I'll tell you something. Something I've never told another living soul. I never did enjoy it the way some women . . . say they do.

CORA   Lottie! You?

LOTTIE   Why do you say *me* like that? Because I talk kinda dirty at times? But that's all it is, is talk. I talk all the time just to convince myself that I'm alive. And I stuff myself with victuals just to feel I've got something inside me. And I'm full of all kinds of crazy curiosity about . . . all the things in life I seem to have missed out on. Now I'm telling you the truth, Cora. Nothing ever really happened to me while it was going on.

CORA Lottie . . .

LOTTIE That first night Morris and I were together, right after we were married, when we were in bed together for the first time, after it was all over, and he had fallen asleep, I lay there in bed wondering what in the world all the cautioning had been about. Nothing had happened to me at all, and I though Mama and Papa musta been makin' things up.

CORA Oh, Lottie!

LOTTIE So, don't come to me for sympathy, Cora. I'm not the person to give it to you.
(*Outside there is a low rumble of thunder.* SONNY *enters from the dining room with a cup of flour paste and his scrapbook.* MORRIS *returns from his walk, his face mysterious and grave*)

MORRIS We'd better be starting back now, honey. It looks like rain.

CORA Oh, don't talk about leaving. Can't you and Lottie stay all night? I'd get up early and fix you breakfast. I'll fix you biscuits.

MORRIS I can't, Cora. I got patients coming first thing in the morning.

LOTTIE And I have to go home to let out the cats.

MORRIS It was a wonderful dinner, Cora.

CORA Thank you, Morris.

LOTTIE (*On a sudden impulse, she springs to her feet, hoists her skirt to her waist, and begins wrestling with her corset*) My God, I'm gonna take off this corset and ride back home in comfort.

CORA (*Runs protectively to* SONNY, *and stands between him and* LOTTIE, *to prevent his seeing this display*) Sonny! Turn your head.

LOTTIE   My God! That feels good. (*She rolls the corset under her arm and rubs the flesh on her stomach in appreciation of its new freedom. Then she reaches for the bag of fried chicken*)   Thanks for the fried chicken, Cora. Oh, good! A gizzard. (*She brings out a gizzard to gnaw on*) It was a wonderful dinner. You're a better cook than I am.

CORA   That's not so.

LOTTIE   Kiss me good-bye, Sonny.

SONNY   Good-bye, Aunt Lottie.

LOTTIE   (*Hugging him close*)   Good night, darling.

MORRIS   That was a fine recitation, Edwin Booth.

SONNY   Thank you, Uncle Morris.

LOTTIE   (*Facing her husband with a bright smile, as though nothing but happiness had ever passed between them*)   I'm ready, Daddy.

MORRIS   All right, Mama. Good of you to have us, Cora.

CORA   Glad you could come, Morris.

LOTTIE   (*At the door, thinks of one last piece of news she must impart to her sister before leaving*)   Oh, Cora! I forgot to tell you. Mamie Keeler's in the hospital.

MORRIS   (*Goes out on the porch now*)   Look like it's gonna rain any minute now.

CORA   What's wrong?

LOTTIE   Some kind of female trouble.

CORA   Oh . . . that's too bad.
(*But LOTTIE can tell by the sound of CORA's voice that she is too preoccupied now with her own worries to care about Mamie Keeler*)

LOTTIE   Oh, God, Cora . . . I just can't go off and leave you this way.

CORA   I'll be all right, Lottie.

LOTTIE   Look, Cora . . . if you and the kids wanta come over and stay with us . . . we'll manage somehow . . .

CORA   Oh, thank you, Lottie. (*They embrace as though recognizing the bond of their blood*) But I'm going to work this out for myself, Lottie.

LOTTIE   Good-bye, Cora.

MORRIS   (*From outside*)   It's beginning to rain, honey.

LOTTIE   (*Hurrying out the door*)   Hold your horses, Morris. I'm coming. Don't be impatient now. (*They exit. Now* CORA *returns to the center of the room, feeling somehow deserted*)

SONNY   It's always so quiet after company leaves, isn't it?

CORA   Hush, Sonny. I'm trying to think.
(*From outside, we hear the sound of* MORRIS' *car driving off, and then the sound of the rain and the wind*)

SONNY   Let's move to California, Mom. Please, let's move to California.
(*But* CORA *has made a sudden decision. She rushes to the telephone*)

CORA   Long distance. (*A moment's wait*) This is Mrs. Flood, three-two-one. I want to talk to Mr. Rubin Flood at the Hotel Boomerang in Blackwell . . . Yes, I'll wait.

SONNY   (*In an innocent voice*)   I bet he isn't there. I bet anything.

CORA   Hello? He isn't? Would you ask them if he's been there this week? (*A moment's wait*) He hasn't! Oh . . . Well, please tell him, if he does come, to call his family immediately. It's very important.

(*A fallen expression on her face, she sits for a moment,
wondering what next move to make. Then she hears a car
approaching from the distance. She jumps up and runs to
the window*)

SONNY   It isn't Dad. I can always tell the sound of his car.
(CORA *comes back to the middle of the room*)

CORA   Run along to bed now, Sonny. It's late. I have to go
out and empty the pan under the ice box.
(CORA *goes out through the dining-room door.* SONNY
*walks slowly, hesitantly, to the foot of the stairs and stands
there, looking up at the blackness at the top. He stands
there several moments, unable to force himself to go further. From the kitchen we hear* CORA'S *muffled sobs.* SONNY
cries out in fear)

SONNY   Mom!
(CORA *returns now, not wanting* SONNY *to know she has
been crying*)

CORA   Sonny, I though I told you to go upstairs. (*She looks
at him now and sees his embarrassed fear*) Sonny, why are
you so afraid of the dark?

SONNY   'Cause . . . you can't see what's in front of you.
And it might be something awful.

CORA   You're the man of the house now, Sonny. You mustn't
be afraid.

SONNY   I'm not afraid . . . if someone's with me.
(CORA *walks over to him and takes his hand*)

CORA   Come, boy. We'll go up together.
(*They start up the stairs to face the darkness hovering
there like an omen*)

CURTAIN

Act Three

SCENE: *It is the next day, late afternoon. Outside, there is a drizzling rain that has continued through the day.* REENIE *has not dressed all day. She sits by the fire in her robe, rubbing her freshtly shampooed hair with a towel.* CORA *enters from the dining room, wearing a comfortable old kimono. She looks at the tray by* REENIE'S *side.*

CORA   Reenie! is that all you feel like eating?

REENIE   Yes.

CORA   But that's all you've had all day, Reenie. You don't eat enough to keep a bird alive.

REENIE   I . . . I'm not hungry, Mom.

CORA   Now quit feeling sorry for yourself, just because you didn't have a good time last night.

REENIE   Mom, is Dad coming back?

CORA   I don't know. I tried to call him last night but couldn't get him.

REENIE   Aren't you mad at him any more?

CORA   No . . . I'm not mad.

REENIE   Even though he hit you?

CORA   Even though he hit me. I was defying him to do it . . . and he did. I can't blame him now.

REENIE   Do you think he *will* be back, Mom?

CORA   This is the day he was supposed to come back. It's almost suppertime and he still isn't here.

REENIE   But it's been raining, Mom. I'll bet the roads are bad.

CORA   You love your father, don't you?

REENIE   Yes.

CORA   Well, I'm glad. The people we love aren't always perfect, are they? But if we love them, we have to take them as they are. After all, I guess I'm not perfect, either.

REENIE   You are too, Mom. You're absolutely perfect, in every way.

CORA   No, I'm not, Reenie. I . . . I have my own score to settle for. I've always accused your father of neglecting you kids, but maybe I've hurt you more with pampering. You . . . and Sonny, too.

REENIE   What do you mean, Mom?

CORA   Oh, nothing. I can't say anything more about it right now. Forget it. (*For some reason we don't yet know, she tries to change the subject*) Are you feeling a little better now?

REENIE   I guess so.

CORA   Well, the world isn't going to end just because your young man went off and left you.

REENIE   Oh, Mom. It was the most humiliating thing that ever happened to me.

CORA   Where do you think Sammy went?

REENIE   He went out to the cars at intermission time with some other girl.

CORA   To spoon?

REENIE   They call it *necking*.

CORA   Are you sure of this?

REENIE   Mom, that's what all the boys do at intermission time. They take girls and go out to the cars. Some of them don't even come back for the rest of the dance.

CORA   But are you sure Sammy did that? Did you see him?

REENIE   No, Mom. I just know that's what he did.

CORA   Wouldn't *you* have gone out to one of the cars with him?

REENIE   (*With self-disparagement*)   Oh. Mom.

CORA   What makes you say "Oh, Mom" that way?

REENIE   He wouldn't have liked *me* that way.

CORA   But why? Why not?

REENIE   I'm just not *hot stuff* like the other girls.

CORA   Reenie, what an expression! You're pretty. You're every bit as pretty as Flirt or Mary Jane. Half a woman's beauty is in her confidence.

REENIE   Oh, Mom.

CORA   Reenie, I've tried to raise you proper, but . . . you're sixteen now. It's perfectly natural if a boy wants to kiss you, and you let him. It's all right if you *like* the boy.

REENIE   (*A hesitant admission*)   Oh . . . Sammy kissed me.

CORA   (*Quite surprised*)   He did?

REENIE   On the way out to the party, in Punky's car. Flirt and Punky were in the front seat, Sammy and I in the back. Punky had a flask . . .

CORA   The little devil!

REENIE   Mom, most of those wealthy boys who go away to school are kind of wild.

CORA   Go on.

REENIE   Well, Punky and Flirt started necking, very first

thing. Flirt, I don't mean to be tattling, but she *is* kind of fast.

CORA   I guessed as much. You aren't tattling.

REENIE   Well, Sammy and I felt kind of embarrassed, with no one else to talk to, and so he took my hand. Oh, he was very nice about it, Mom. And then he put an arm around me, and said . . . "May I kiss you, Reenie?" And I was so surprised, I said yes before I knew *what* I was saying. And he kissed me. Was it all right, Mom?

CORA   Did you like the young man? That's the important thing.

REENIE   Yes, I . . . I liked him . . . very much. (*She sobs helplessly*) Oh, Mom.

CORA   There, there, Reenie dear. If he's the kind of young man who goes around kissing all the girls, you don't want to worry about him any more. You did right to leave the party!

REENIE   Did I, Mom?

CORA   Of course you did. I'm very disappointed in Sammy. I thought he was such a nice boy. But I guess appearances can be deceiving.

REENIE   Oh Mom!

CORA   There, there, dear. There are plenty of other young men in the world. You're young. You're not going to have to worry.

REENIE   (*Struggling to her feet*)   Mom, I don't think I ever want to get married.

CORA   Reenie!

REENIE   I mean it, Mom.

CORA   You're too young to make a decision like that.

REENIE   I'm serious.

CORA   What makes you say such a thing? Tell me.

REENIE   I don't want to fight with anyone, like you and
Daddy.

CORA   Oh, God.

REENIE   Every time you and Daddy fight, I just feel that
the whole house is going to cave in all around me.

CORA   Then I *am* to blame.

REENIE   And I think I'd be lots happier, just by myself,
teaching school, or working in an office building.

CORA   No, daughter. You need someone after you grow up.
You need someone.

REENIE   But I don't want to. I don't *want* to need anyone,
ever in my life. It's a horrible feeling to need someone.

CORA   (*Disturbed*)   Daughter!

REENIE   Anyway, the only times I'm really happy are when
I'm alone, practicing at the piano or studying in the library.

CORA   Weren't you happy last night when Sammy kissed you?

REENIE   I guess you can't count on happiness like that.

CORA   Daughter, when you start getting older, you'll find
yourself getting lonely and you'll want someone; someone
who'll hear you if you get sick and cry out in the night;
and someone to give you love and let you give your love
back to him in return. Oh, I'd hate to see any child of mine
miss that in life. (*There is a moment of quiet realization
between them. Then we hear the sound of a car drawing up
to the house.* CORA, *running to the window, is as excited as
a girl*) That must be your father! No, it's Sonny. In a big
limousine. He's getting out of the car as if he owned it. Mrs.
Stanford must have sent him home with her chauffeur.

(*She gives "chauffeur" its American pronunciation.* SONNY, *in his Sunday suit, bursts into the house waving a five-dollar bill in his mother's face*)

SONNY   Mom. Look, Mom! Mrs. Stanford gave me five dollars for speaking my piece. See? Five whole dollars. She said I was the most talented little boy she ever saw. See, Mom? Then she got out her pocketbook and gave me five whole dollars. See?

CORA   I declare. Why, Sonny, I'm proud of you, boy. That's the very first money you ever earned, and I'm very proud.

SONNY   And Mrs. Stanford sent me home with her chauffeur, too, Mom. (*He gives the word its French pronunciation*) That's the way you're supposed to pronounce it, chauf*feur*. It's French.

CORA   If you spend any more time at Mrs. Stanford's, you'll be getting too high-hat to come home. (*She notices* REENIE *starting upstairs*) We'll talk later, Reenie. (REENIE *exits.* CORA *again turns her attention to* SONNY) Did you have anything to eat?

SONNY   Oh, Mom, it was just delicious. She had all kinds of little sandwiches. Gee, they were good. And cocoa, too, Mom, with lots of whipped cream on top, in little white cups with gold edges. Gee, they were pretty. And lots of little cakes, too, with pink frosting and green. And ice cream, too. I just ate and ate and ate.

CORA   Good. That means I won't have to get you any supper.

SONNY   No. I don't want any supper. I'm going to the movies tonight. And to the Royal Candy Kitchen afterwards, to buy myself a great big sundae with chocolate and marshmallow and cherries and . . .

CORA   Now, wait a minute, Sonny. This is the first money you've ever earned in your life, and I think you should save it.

SONNY   Oh, Mom!

CORA   I mean it. Five dollars is a lot of money, and I'm not going to let you squander it on movies and sundaes. You'll thank me for this some day.
(*She takes his piggy bank from the bookcase*)

SONNY   I will not. I will not thank you!

CORA   Sonny.
(*She takes the bill from him and drops it into the bank.* SONNY *is wild at the injustice*)

SONNY   Look what you've done. I hate you! I wanta see the movie. I've just gotta see the movie. If I can't see the movie, I'll kill myself.

CORA   Such foolish talk!

SONNY   I mean it. I'll kill myself.

CORA   Now, be quiet, Sonny. I want to have a little talk.

SONNY   Can I sell the milk bottles for money?

CORA   No! Now quit pestering me about the movies. You've already talked me into letting you see one movie this week. I have scarcely any money now, and I can't spare a cent.
(SONNY *is badly frustrated. He finds the favors that* SAMMY *promised him, displayed on the settee. He throws a handful of confetti recklessly into the air, then dons a paper hat, and blows violently on a paper horn*) Sonny! Stop that racket! You're going to have to clean up that mess.

SONNY   You won't let me have any fun at all.

CORA   The young man was very thoughtful to have sent you the favors. I wish he had been as thoughtful in other ways.

SONNY   Didn't Reenie have a good time at the party last night?

CORA   No.

SONNY   Serves her right. Serves her right.

CORA   Sonny! I'm not going to have any more talk like that.
If you and your sister can't get along, you can at least have
a little respect for one another. Now, come here, Sonny, I
want to talk serious for a little while. (SONNY *taunts her
with the horn*) Will you go sit down?

SONNY   What's the matter?
(*He sits opposite her at the table*)

CORA   Nothing. I just want to talk a while.

SONNY   (*Suddenly solemn and apprehensive*)   Have I done
something bad?

CORA   Well, I don't know if you have or if I have. Anyway,
we've got to talk about it. Sonny, you mustn't come crawling into my bed any more. I let you do it last night, but I
shouldn't have. It was wrong.

SONNY   I was scared.

CORA   Just the same, that's not to happen again, Sonny. It's
not the same when a boy your age comes crawling into bed
with his mother. You can't expect me to mean as much to
you as when you were a baby. Can you understand, Sonny?
(*He looks away from her with unconscious guilt. She
studies him*) I think you're older in your feelings than I
ever realized. You're a funny mixture, Sonny. In some
ways, shy as your sister. In other ways, bold as a pirate.

SONNY   I don't like you any more at all.

CORA   Sonny!

SONNY   I don't care. You make me mad.

CORA   (*Going to him*)   Oh, God, I've kept you too close to
me, Sonny. Too close. I'll take the blame, boy. But don't be
mad. You mother still loves you, Sonny. (*But she sees that
they are at an impasse*) Well, we won't talk about it any
more. Run along to the store now, before it closes. (*We see*

FLIRT'S *face in the door window. She is knocking on the door and calling for* REENIE. CORA *hurries to let her in*) Flirt!

FLIRT (*Rushing inside*) Where's Reenie? Reenie . . . Reenie. Oh, Mrs. Flood, I have the most awful news.

CORA What is it, Flirt?

FLIRT (FLIRT'S *face, her whole body are contorted by shock and confused grief*) Oh, it's so awful.

CORA Tell me.

FLIRT Is Reenie here? I've got to tell her, too.

CORA (*Calls upstairs*) Reenie, can you come down? Flirt is here.

REENIE (*off*) I'm coming.

FLIRT Oh, Mrs. Flood, it's the most awful thing that ever happened in this town. It's the most awful thing I ever heard of happening anywhere.

CORA Did something happen to you, or your family? . . .

FLIRT No, it's Sammy.

CORA Sammy? . . .

REENIE (*Coming downstairs*) What is it, Flirt?

FLIRT Kid! Sammy Goldenbaum . . . killed himself.
(*There is a long silence*)

CORA Where did you hear this, Flirt?

FLIRT Mrs. Givens told me. The hotel people over in Oklahoma City called her about it just a little while ago. They found a letter in Sammy's suitcase Mrs. Givens had written him, inviting him to come home with Punky.

CORA   Oklahoma City?

FLIRT   He went over there last night after he left the party. He took the midnight train. That's what they figured out, because he registered at the hotel this morning at two o'clock.

CORA   How ... did he do it, Flirt?

FLIRT   (*Hides her face in her hands as though hiding from the hideous reality of it*)   He ... Oh, I just can't.

CORA   There, there, honey.

FLIRT   Oh, I'm such a silly about things. He ... he jumped out of the window ... on the fourteenth floor ... and landed on the pavement below.

CORA   Oh, my God.

FLIRT   Oh ... it's really the most terrible thing that ever happened to me. I never did know anyone who killed himself before.

CORA   Does anyone have any idea what made him do it?

FLIRT   No! Punky says that he used to get kind of moody at times, but Punky never expected him to do anything like *this*.

CORA   Why did he go to Oklahoma City in the middle of the night?

FLIRT   No one knows that either ... for sure. But one thing did happen at the party. He was dancing with Mary Jane Ralston ... that cow ... just before intermission ... and Mrs Ralston ... she'd had too much to drink ... comes out in the middle of the floor and stops them.

CORA   What for?

FLIRT   Well, you know how Mrs. Ralston is. No one takes her very serious even if she does have money. Anyway, she came right out in the middle of the floor and gave Sammy a bawling out . . .

CORA   A bawling out? Why?

FLIRT   She said she wasn't giving this party for Jews, and she didn't intend for her daughter to dance with a Jew, and besides, Jews weren't allowed in the country club anyway. And that's not so. They are too allowed in the country club. Maybe they're not permitted to be members, but they're certainly allowed as guests. Everyone knows that. (*she turns now to* REENIE, *who has sat numb in a chair since* FLIRT'S *shocking announcement*) Where were you when it all happened?

REENIE   I . . . I . . .
(*But she is inarticulate*)

CORA   Reenie wasn't feeling well. She left the party and came home.

FLIRT   The other kids told me Sammy was looking for you everywhere. He was going around asking everyone, Where's Reenie?

CORA   That . . . that's too bad.

FLIRT   (*Turning to* CORA) . . . But a thing like that isn't serious enough to make a boy kill himself, is it?

CORA   Well . . . he did.

FLIRT   An old blabbermouth like Mrs. Ralston?

CORA   She was a stranger to Sammy. She probably sounded like the voice of the world.

FLIRT   Gee . . . I just don't understand things like that. Do you know something else, Mrs. Flood? They called Sammy's mother way out in California, and told her, and I guess she was terribly sorry and everything, but she told them to go on and have the funeral in Oklahoma City, that she'd pay all the expenses, but she wouldn't be able to come for it because she was working. And she cried over the telephone and asked them please to try and keep her name out of the papers, because she said it wasn't generally known that she had a son.

CORA   There won't be anyone Sammy knows at the funeral, will there?

FLIRT   Mrs. Givens said Punky and his daddy could drive us over for it. Will you come, Reenie? (REENIE *nods*) Do you wanta come, too, Sonny? (SONNY *nods*) Well . . . it'll be day after tomorrow, in the afternoon. We'll all have to get excused from school. Oh, gee, it all makes me feel so kind of *strange*. Doesn't it *you*, kid? I think I'll go to Sunday School tomorrow. Do you wanta go with me, Reenie? (REENIE *nods yes*) Oh, I feel just terrible.
(FLIRT *bolts out the front door, as though wanting to run away from all that is tragic or sorrowful in life.* CORA *keeps silent for several moments, her eyes on* REENIE)

CORA   Where were you when Sammy went off?

REENIE   (*Twisting with grief*)   Stop it, Mom!

CORA   Tell me. Where were you?

REENIE   Don't, Mom!

CORA   (*Commanding*)   *Tell* me.

REENIE   I . . . was up in . . . the girls' room.

CORA   Where did you leave Sammy?

REENIE   As soon as we got to the party, Sammy and I started dancing. He danced three straight dances with me, Mom. Nobody cut in. I didn't think anybody was ever going to cut in, Mom. I got to feeling so humiliated I didn't know what to do. I just couldn't bear for Sammy to think that no one liked me.

CORA   Dear God!

REENIE   So I told Sammy there was someone at the party

I had to talk to. Then I took him over to Mary Jane Ralston and . . . introduced him to her . . . and told him to dance with her.

CORA   Reenie!

REENIE   I . . . I thought he'd like her.

CORA   But you said that *you* liked Sammy. You told me you did.

REENIE   But, Mom, I just couldn't *bear* for him to think I was such a wallflower.

CORA   You ran off and *hid*, when an ounce of thoughtfulness, one or two kind words, might have saved him.

REENIE   I didn't *know*. I didn't *know*.

CORA   A nice young man like that, bright and pleasant, handsome as a prince, caught out here in this sandy soil without a friend to his name and no one to turn to when some thoughtless fool attacks him and he takes it to heart. (REENIE *sobs uncontrollably*) Tears aren't going to do any good now, Reenie. Now, you listen to me. I've heard all I intend to listen to about being so shy and sensitive and afraid of people. I can't respect those feelings any more. They're nothing but selfishness. (REENIE *starts to bolt from the room, just as* FLIRT *did, but* CORA'S *voice holds her*) Reenie! It's a fine thing when we have so little confidence in ourselves, we can't stop to think of the other person.

SONNY   (*Who has been a silent listener until now*)   I *hate* people.

CORA   Sonny!

SONNY   I *do*.

CORA   Then you're just as bad as Peg Ralston.

SONNY   How can you keep from hating?

CORA   There are all kinds of people in the world. And you
have to live with them all. God never promised us any
different. The bad people, you don't hate. You're only
sorry they have to be. Now, run along to the store before
it closes.
(SONNY *goes out, and finds himself again confronted by
the jeers of the neighborhood boys, which sound like the
voices that have plagued humanity from the beginning of
time*)

BOYS' VOICES
Sissy Sonny!
Sonny Flood! His name is mud!
Sonny plays with dolls!
Sonny loves his mama!
(*Hearing the voices,* CORA *runs to the door, but stops
herself from going further*)

CORA   I guess I can't go through life protecting him from
bullies. (*She goes to* REENIE) I'm sorry I spoke so harshly
to you, Reenie.

REENIE   He asked for *me* . . . for *me*. The only time anyone ever *wanted* me, or *needed* me, in my entire life. And
I wasn't there. I didn't stop once to think of . . . Sammy.
I've always thought I was the only person in the world who
had any feelings at all.

CORA   Well . . . you're not, if that's any comfort. Where
are you going, dear?

REENIE (*Resignedly*)   I haven't done anything to my room
all day. I . . . I still have to make my bed.
(REENIE *exits upstairs*)

CORA (*Calling after her*)   It's Saturday. Change the linens.
I put them in the attic to dry. (CORA *goes into the parlor
to pull down the shades.* RUBIN *enters from the dining
room. He is in his stocking feet, and is carrying several
bags, which he drops onto the floor with a clatter.* CORA
comes running from the parlor) My God!

RUBIN   I scare ya?

CORA   Rubin! I hate to be frightened so.

RUBIN   I din *mean* to frighten ya.

CORA   I didn't hear you drive in.

RUBIN   I didn't.

CORA   Where's the car.

RUBIN   It ain't runnin' right. Left it downtown at the garage. I walked home.

CORA   Why did you come in the back way?

RUBIN   Cora, what difference does it make if I come in the
back way or the front way, or down the chimney? My
boots was covered with mud. So I left 'em out on the back
porch. I din wanta track up your nice, clean house. Now,
wasn't that thoughtful of me?

CORA   Did you get my message?

RUBIN   What message?

CORA   (*A little haughty*)   Oh . . . nothing.

RUBIN   What message you talkin' about?

CORA   The route you left me said you'd be in Blackwell last
night. I called you there, but . . . Well, I suppose you
had better places to be.

RUBIN   That's right. I did. What'd ya call me for?

CORA   (*Hurt*)   I don't know now. You'll be wanting a hot
bath. I'll go turn on the water tank. (CORA *exits through
dining-room door.* RUBIN *sits in his big chair and drops his
face into his hands with a look of sad discouragement.
Then he begins to unpack one of the bags, taking out small
pieces of harness and tossing them on the floor. In a few
moments,* CORA *returns*)   What made you decide to come
back?

RUBIN   I lost my job.

CORA   What?

RUBIN   I said I lost my job.

CORA   Rubin! You've always sold more harness for the company than any of the other salesmen.

RUBIN   Yah. The on'y trouble is, *no* one's selling much harness today because no one's buyin' it. People are buyin' automobiles. Harness salesmen are . . . things of the past.

CORA   Do you mean . . . your company's going out of business?

RUBIN   That's it! You won the kewpie doll.

CORA   Oh, Rubin!

RUBIN   So that's why ya couldn't get me in Blackwell last night. I went somewhere else, regardless of what you were thinkin', lookin' for a job.

CORA   (*A little embarrassed with regret*)   Oh . . . I apologize, Rubin.

RUBIN   Oh, that's all right. You have to get in your li'l digs ev'ry once in a while. I'm used to 'em.

CORA   I'm really awfully sorry. Believe me.

RUBIN   I was in Tulsa, talkin' to some men at the Southwest Supply Company. They're hirin' lotsa new men to go out in the fields and sell their equipment.

CORA   (*Seizing her opportunity*)   Rubin Flood, now that you've lost one traveling job, I'm not going to let you take another. You go downtown the first thing Monday morning and talk to John Fraser. He's bought out all the Curley Cue markets in town, and he needs men to manage them. He'd give you a job in a minute. Now, you do what I say, Rubin.

RUBIN (*He looks at her for several moments before getting to his feet*) God damn! I come home here t'apologize to you for hittin' ya. I been feelin' all week like the meanest critter alive, because I took a sock at a woman. My wife, at that. I walked in here ready to *beg* ya to forgive me. Now I feel like doin' it all over again. Don't you realize you can't talk to a man like that? Don't you realize that every time you talk that way, I just gotta go out and raise more hell, just to prove to myself I'm a free man? Don't you know that when you talk to a man like that, you're not givin' him credit for havin' any brains, or any guts, or a spine, or . . . or a few other body parts that are pretty important, too? All these years we been married, you never once really admitted to yourself what kinda man I am. No, ya keep talkin' to me like I was the kinda man you think I *oughta* be. (*He grabs her by the shoulders*) Look at me. Don't you know who I am? Don't you know who I am?

CORA Rubin, you're hurting me.

RUBIN I'm takin' the job if I can get it. It's a damn good job, pays good money.

CORA I don't care about money.

RUBIN No, you don't! Not until you see Peg Ralston come waltzin' down the street in a new fur coat, and then you start wonderin' why old Rubin don't shoot hisself in the foot to make a lot of money.

CORA Rubin, I promise you I'll never envy Peg Ralston another thing, as long as I live.

RUBIN Did it ever occur to you that maybe I feel like a cheapskate because I can't buy you no fur coat? Did you ever stop to think maybe I'd like to be able to send my kids away to a fine college?

CORA All I'm asking is for you to give them something of *yourself.*

RUBIN God damn it! What have *I* got to give 'em? In this day and age, what's a man like me got to give? With the whole world so all-fired crazy about makin' money, how can *any* man, unless he's got a million dollars stuck in his pocket, feel he's got anything else to give that's very important?

CORA   Rubin!

RUBIN   I mean it, Cora.

CORA   I never realized you had such doubts.

RUBIN   The new job is work I've never done. Work I never even thought of doin'. Learnin' about all that goddamn machinery, and how to get out there and demonstrate it. Working with different kinds of men, that's smarter than I am, that think fast and talk sharp and mean all business. Men I can't sit around and chew tobacco with and joke with like I did m'old customers. I . . . I don't like 'em. I don't know if I'm *gonna* like them.

CORA   But you just said you wanted the job.

RUBIN   I don't like them, but I'm gonna join them. A fellow's gotta get into the swim. There's nothing else to do. But I'm scared. I don't know how I'll make out. I . . . I'm scared.

CORA   I never supposed you had it *in* you to fear.

RUBIN   I s'pose all this time you been thinkin' you was married to one a them movin'-pitcher fellas that jump off bridges and hold up trains and shoot Indians, and are never scared a nothin'. Times are changin', Cora, and I dunno where they're goin'. When I was a boy, there wasn't much more to this town than a post office. I on'y had six years a schoolin' cause that's all the Old Man thought I'd ever need. Now look at things. School buildin's, churches, fine stores, movie theatres, a country club. Men becomin' millionaires overnight, drivin' down the street in big limousines, goin' out to the country club and gettin' drunk, acting like they was the lords of creation. I dunno what to think of things now, Cora. I'm a stranger in the very land I was born in.

CORA (*Trying to restore his pride*) Your folks pioneered this country.

RUBIN Sometimes I wonder if it's not a lot easier to pioneer a country than it is to settle down in it. I look at the town now and don't recognize anything in it. I come home here, and I still have to get used to the piano, and the telephone, and the gas stove, and the lace curtains at the windows, the carpets on the floor. All these things are still *new* to me. I dunno what to make of 'em. How can *I* feel I've got anything to give to my children when the world's as strange to me as it is to them?

CORA (*With a new awareness of him*) Rubin!

RUBIN I'm doin' the best I can, Cora. Can't ya understand that? I'm doin' the best I can.

CORA Yes, Rubin. I know you are.

RUBIN Now, there's a few more things I gotta say . . . I wanna apologize. I'm sorry I hit ya, Cora. I'm awful sorry.

CORA I know I provoked you, Rubin.

RUBIN You provoked me, but . . . I still shouldn'ta hit ya. It wasn't manly.

CORA I'm not holding it against you, Rubin.

RUBIN And I'm sorry I made such a fuss about you gettin' the girl a new dress. But I was awful worried about losin' my job then, and I din have much money left in the bank.

CORA Rubin, if I'd known that, I wouldn't have *thought* of buying the dress. You should have told me, Rubin.

RUBIN I din wanta make you worry, too.

CORA   But that's what I'm for.

RUBIN   That's all I gotta say, Cora, except that . . . I love ya. You're a good woman and I couldn't git along without you.

CORA   I love you, too, Rubin. And I couldn't get along without you another day.

RUBIN   You're clean, and dainty. Give a man a feeling of decency . . . and order . . . and respect.

CORA   Thank you, Rubin.

RUBIN   Just don't get the idea you can rearrange *me* like ya do the house, whenever ya wanta put it in order.

CORA   I'll remember. (*There is a short silence between them now, filled with new understanding*) When you have fears about things, please tell me, Rubin.

RUBIN   It's hard for a man t'admit his fears, even to hisself.

CORA   Why? Why?

RUBIN   He's always afraid of endin' up like . . . like your brother-in-law Morris.

CORA   Oh!
(CORA *has a new appreciation of him. She runs to him, throwing her arms about him in a fast embrace. A glow of satisfaction radiates from* RUBIN, *to have his woman back in his arms*)

RUBIN   Oh, my goodness. (RUBIN *carries* CORA *center, where they sit like honeymooners, she on his lap; and he kisses her.* SONNY *returns now with a sack of groceries, and stands staring at his parents until they become aware of him*) H'lo, son.

SONNY   Hi!

CORA   Take the groceries to the kitchen, Sonny. (*Obediently,*

SONNY *starts for the dining-room door*) Rubin, Mrs. Stanford paid Sonny five dollars this afternoon for speaking a piece at her tea party.

RUBIN   I'll be damned. He'll be makin' more money than his Old Man.
(SONNY *exits now through dining-room door*)

CORA   Be nice to him, Rubin. Show him you want to be his friend.

RUBIN   I'm nice to that boy, ain't I?

CORA   Sometimes you do talk awfully rough and bad-natured.

RUBIN   Well ... *life's* rough. *Life's* bad-natured.

CORA   I know. And I keep trying to pretend it isn't.

RUBIN   I'll remind ya.

CORA   Every time I see the kids go out of the house, I worry ... like I was watching them go out into life, and they seem so young and helpless.

RUBIN   But ya gotta let 'em go, Cora. Ya can't hold 'em.

CORA   I've always felt I could give them life like a present, all wrapped in white, with every promise of happiness inside.

RUBIN   That ain't the way it works.

CORA   No. All I can promise them is life itself. (*With this realization, she gets off* RUBIN's *lap*) I'd better go to the kitchen and put the groceries away.

RUBIN   (*Grabs her to him, not willing to let her go*)   T'hell with the groceries!

CORA   (*A maidenly protest*)   Rubin!

RUBIN (*Caressing her*)   Is there any chance of us bein' alone t'night?

CORA (*Secretively*)   I think Reenie plans to go to the library. If you give Sonny a dime, I'm sure he'll go to the movies.

RUBIN   It's a deal.
(*He tries again to re-engage her in lovemaking*)

CORA   Now, Rubin, be patient.
(*She exits through the dining-room door as* REENIE *comes running downstairs*)

REENIE   Did I hear Daddy?

RUBIN   Hello, daughter.

REENIE (*She runs into his arms and he lifts her high in the air*)   Oh, Daddy!

RUBIN   Well, how's my girl?

REENIE   I feel better now that you're home, Daddy.

RUBIN   Thank ya, daughter.

REENIE   I've been practicing a new piece, Daddy. It's Chopin. Do you want me to play it for you?

RUBIN   Sure. I like sweet music same as anyone.

REENIE   I can't play it quite perfect yet, but almost.
(REENIE *goes into parlor and in a moment we hear another wistful piece by Chopin*)

RUBIN   That's all right. (SONNY *now returns and stands far right.* RUBIN, *center, faces him. They look at each other with wonder and just a little resentment. But* RUBIN *goes to* SONNY, *making the effort to offer himself*) Son, your mom tells me you do real well, goin' around speaking pieces, gettin' to be a reg'lar Jackie Coogan. I got a customer has a daughter does real well at that kinda thing. Gets up before people and whistles.

SONNY Whistles?

RUBIN Yah! Like birds. Every kinda bird ya ever heard of.
Maybe you'd like to meet her sometime.

SONNY Oh, maybe.
(RUBIN *feels himself on uncertain ground with his son*)

RUBIN Your mom said maybe you'd like to go to the movie
tonight. I guess I could spare you the money.
(*He digs into his pocket*)

SONNY I've changed my mind. I don't want to now.
(SONNY *turns from his father*)

RUBIN (*Looks at his son as though realizing sadly the
breech between them. With a feeling of failure, he puts a
warm hand on* SONNY'S *shoulder*) Oh! Well, I ain't gonna
argue. (*He walks out, and as he passes the parlor, he
speaks to* REENIE) That's real purty, daughter.

REENIE Thank you, Daddy.

RUBIN (*Opens dining-room door and speaks to* CORA) Cora,
those kids ain't goin' to the movies. Come on now.

CORA (*Off*) I'll be up in a minute, Rubin.

RUBIN (*Closing the door behind him, speaking to* REENIE *and*
SONNY) I'm goin' upstairs now, and have my bath.
(REENIE *and* SONNY *watch him all the way as he goes up-
stairs*)

SONNY They always want to be alone.

REENIE All married people do, crazy.
(SONNY *impulsively sticks out his tongue at her. But she
ignores him, picking up one of the favors, a reminder of*
SAMMY, *and fondling it tenderly.* SONNY *begins to feel regret*)

SONNY I'm sorry I made a face at you, Reenie.

REENIE (*Sobbing softly*)   Go on and make as many faces as you like. I'm not going to fight with you any more.

SONNY   Don't cry, Reenie.

REENIE I didn't know Sammy had even remembered the favors until I started to go. Then I went to find my coat, and there they were, sticking out of my pocket. At the very moment he was putting them there . . . he must have had in mind doing what he did.

SONNY (*With a burst of new generosity*)   *You! You* keep the favors, Reenie.

REENIE He promised them to *you.*

SONNY   Just the same . . . *you* keep them, Reenie.

REENIE Do you mean it?

SONNY   Yes.

REENIE You never were thoughtful like this . . . before. (CORA *comes through the dining-room door now, hears the children's plans, and stands unobserved, listening*)

SONNY   Reenie, do you want to go to the movie tonight? It's Mae Murray in *Fascination,* and there's an *Our Gang Comedy* first.

REENIE I don't feel I should.

SONNY   When I feel bad, I just *have* to go to the movies. I just *have* to.

REENIE I was supposed to go to the library tonight.

SONNY   Please go with me, Reenie. Please.

REENIE Do you really want me?

SONNY   Yes, Reenie. Yes.

REENIE   Where would you get the money to take *me*, Sonny?
I have to pay adult admission. It's thirty-five cents.

SONNY   I've got all the money we'll need.
(*He runs for his piggy bank as* CORA *makes a quick return
to the dining room*)

REENIE   Sonny! Mother told you you had to save that money.

SONNY   I don't care. She's not going to boss me for the rest
of my life. It's *my* money, and I've got a right to spend it.
(*With a heroic gesture of defiance, he throws the piggy
bank smashing against the fireplace, its pieces scattering on
the floor*)

REENIE   Sonny!

SONNY   (*Finding his five-dollar bill in the rubble*)   And we'll
have enough for popcorn, too, and for ice cream afterwards at the Royal Candy Kitchen.
(*Now we see* CORA *in the parlor again, a silent witness*)

REENIE   I feel very proud to be treated by my little brother.

SONNY   Let's hurry. The comedy starts at seven o'clock and
I don't want to miss it.

REENIE   We can stay for the second show if we miss the
comedy.

SONNY   Oh, I want to stay for the second show, anyway. I
always see the comedy twice.

CORA   (*Coming forth now*)   Are you children going some
place?

REENIE   We're going to the movie, Mom.

CORA   Together?

REENIE   Yes.

CORA   Well . . . that's nice.

REENIE   Darn it. I left my rubbers out on the porch.
   (*She exits*)

RUBIN (*From upstairs*)   Cora!

CORA   I'll be up in a minute, Rubin. (*She turns thoughtfully
   to her son*) Have you forgiven your mother, Sonny?

SONNY (*Inscrutable*)   Oh . . . maybe.

CORA   Your mother still loves you, Sonny.
   (*She puts an arm around him but he avoids her embrace*)

SONNY   Don't, Mom.

CORA   All right. I understand.

RUBIN (*Upstairs, growing more impatient*)   Cora! Come on,
   honey!

CORA (*Calling back to him*)   I'll be up in a minute, Rubin.
   (SONNY *looks at her with accusing eyes*) Good-bye, Sonny!
   (REENIE *sticks her head in the door from outside*)

REENIE   Hurry up, Sonny!

RUBIN   Come on, Cora!
   (CORA *starts up the stairs to her husband, stopping for one
   final look at her departing son. And* SONNY, *just before going out the door, stops for one final look at his mother, his
   face full of confused understanding. Then he hurries out to*
   REENIE, *and* CORA, *like a shy maiden, starts up the stairs,
   where we see* RUBIN'S *naked feet standing in the warm light
   at the top*)

CORA   I'm coming, Rubin. I'm coming.

                                              CURTAIN

BANTAM CLASSICS

NOVELS

(continued on next page)

DRAMA

COLLECTIONS

BIOGRAPHY

NON-FICTION